THE POWER
OF PULSES

DAN JASON,
HILARY MALONE
and
ALISON MALONE
EATHORNE

*With organic-gardening
easy-grow advice
and 50 recipes*

The POWER of Pulses

SAVING THE WORLD
WITH PEAS, BEANS,
CHICKPEAS,
FAVAS & LENTILS

Douglas & McIntyre

Peas, please! The delicious Brazilian Snack Pea in flower form. *Carol Pope photo.*

Page vi photo by Carol Pope

2 3 4 5 — 20 19 18 17 16

DOUGLAS AND MCINTYRE (2013) LTD.
P.O. Box 219, Madeira Park, BC, V0N 2H0
www.douglas-mcintyre.com

Recipes on pages 133, 144–45, 154, 175 by Dan Jason
Photos by Christina Symons except where otherwise noted
Cover photographs by Christina Symons
Food styling by Anna Comfort O'Keeffe and Hilary Malone
Floral pattern by iStock.com/yganko
Edited by Carol Pope and Nicola Goshulak
Indexed by Nicola Goshulak
Text and cover design by Diane Robertson
Printed and bound in Canada

Douglas and McIntyre (2013) Ltd. acknowledges the support of the Canada Council for the Arts, which last year invested $157 million to bring the arts to Canadians throughout the country. We also gratefully acknowledge financial support from the Government of Canada through the Canada Book Fund and from the Province of British Columbia through the BC Arts Council and the Book Publishing Tax Credit.

Cataloguing data available from Library and Archives Canada

ISBN 978-1-77162-102-1 (paper)
ISBN 978-1-77162-103-8 (ebook)

Dedication

This book is dedicated
to all lovers of the land.

Contents

ACKNOWLEDGEMENTS

Special acknowledgement to Carol Pope. Thank you, Carol, for encouraging me to write this book! Thank you for your awesome editing and writing skills and for your friendliness and respectfulness throughout the process.

A special thank you also to Hilary Malone and Alison Malone Eathorne for the fabulous recipes they contributed to this book.

—*Dan Jason*

To our mother, Lorna, for encouraging us to play in the kitchen since we were old enough to hold a whisk. Your unwavering support of our culinary adventures means the world to us.

—*Hilary Malone and Alison Malone Eathorne*

PREFACE

As a long-time food gardener, I've prided myself on trying to grow just about everything worth coaxing out of the ground for the kitchen table. So I was surprised to discover from Dan Jason—a lifelong food activist, bestselling author and founder of Salt Spring Seeds—that I had completely missed out on the delicious and diverse family of pulses.

Who knew that throughout my garden in gorgeous tangles of trellised blooms and pink-striped or purple pods, I could grow a treasure trove of beans, peas, chickpeas, favas and lentils? Yet my spring and summer garden now abounds with pulses: black and white Orca beans, Blue Pod Desiree Peas, Black Beluga Lentils, Chestnut Chickpeas and Crimson-flowered Favas! Who knew that garden-grown pulses have an unforgettable fresh taste and creamy texture? And who knew that *wherever* they grow, these drought-resistant, super-easy dynamos pump nitrogen into the soil, leaving it healthier and more fertile than before?

It's no wonder then that the United Nations' General Assembly has named 2016 the International Year of Pulses. Thanks to their durability, ultra-light ecological footprint and long-lasting benefits to the earth, these hardy, bountiful and remarkably nourishing ancient crops are now lauded as the food of the future. Noted as a vital source of plant-based proteins and amino acids for people around the globe, the UN recommends pulses be eaten regularly to prevent and help manage chronic diseases such as diabetes, coronary conditions and cancer.

And whether you grow your own from scratch or source them from your local market, pulses are amazingly versatile in the kitchen. Award-winning recipe developers and bestselling authors Hilary Malone and Alison Malone Eathorne have cooked up a storm of sumptuous ways to eat pulses every day, with starters like Socca Tart with Olive Tapenade and tasty main dishes, like Crispy Chickpea Power Bowl with Tahini Dressing and Fava Bean and Artichoke Tagliatelle. There's even dessert, from Spiced Navy Bean Pumpkin Pie with Pecan Streusel to Black Bean Brownies with Espresso Ganache. All in all, this beautiful book will help you celebrate the International Year of Pulses in style and leave you inspired, well-fed and well-nourished. Bon appétit!

—*Carol Pope*
  Associate Editor

INTRODUCTION

I have been growing and talking about the value of pulses—dry peas and beans, chickpeas, favas and lentils—for 30 years, and remain more convinced than ever that they could help renew the health of our planet.

Pulses are tried and true—people in temperate climates have been growing and eating them for more than ten thousand years. Nutritional powerhouses, pulses are still the most essential part of the diets of billions of people worldwide.

Belonging to the amazing and prolific legume plant family (Leguminosae or Fabaceae), pulses can snatch nitrogen out of the air and add it to the earth. Because of this powerful ability to increase the fertility of soil by simply growing in it, they are the epitome of renewable energy.

Easy to grow and prepare, dry peas and beans, chickpeas, favas and lentils can be cooked in a seemingly infinite variety of simple and delicious ways and offer much culinary delight because of their diverse tastes and textures. Cultures around the world have created special dishes for all of the pulses, and this book contains 50 inspired recipes that borrow from the best of them.

The surprising news is that even though most North Americans don't know beans about beans, our farmers grow vast acreages of pulses to export to millions of people who do appreciate them. And while Canada is the world's largest exporter of pulses[1], Canadians consume less than 10 percent of what their farmers grow. It is time for Canadians and Americans to

Top and Bottom Right: Chris Thoreau photo. Bottom Left: Photo © Jan Mangan (jmangan@got.net).

realize that pulses—flexible enough to be prepared in hundreds of memorable ways for breakfast, lunch or dinner—could and should constitute a much larger portion of our daily diet. And in addition to buying pulses from our local farmers, we can grow them ourselves easily . . . and organically.

Of all the thousands of years seeds have been handed from farmer to farmer, it's only in the past 50 or so that poisons have been used to grow food. We are at a crucial moment in our story when it is absolutely vital that we return to feeding everyone with clean food and water instead of continuing to play havoc with the health and well-being of ourselves and all the earth's creatures. Pulses can be easily grown without herbicides and pesticides if we size down the North American model of industrial agriculture.

To this day, millions of small farmers grow beans without chemicals. And I have been growing beans myself successfully for 30 years without ever resorting to poisons. Pulses are also light on water, increasingly important on this planet where drought is becoming more and more a daily concern.

Being the nutrient-dense and easy-to-grow foods that they are, pulses can point us in the direction of a safe and sustainable agriculture that gives everyone access to clean food and water, along with the possibility of living in health, harmony and mutual benefit.

Renewable energy is everywhere, every day for the celebrating. Pulse plants can show the way by enabling humans to be renewed by our daily food. Like the pulses within our bodies, they are slow and deep and at the heart of things.

Pulses require between 20 to 40 times less fossil fuel to produce than meat, yet they provide incredible nourishment. And meanwhile, these same pulses regenerate our earth, nourishing the soil that nourishes our food.

I hope this book shows how much power there can be in a handful of beans, and how much delight there is to be had in growing and cooking pulses.

—Dan Jason

Photos © Jan Mangan

CHAPTER 1

Saving the World
WITH PEAS, BEANS, CHICKPEAS, FAVAS AND LENTILS

It's inspiring to think that pulses have been around for more than ten thousand years and what that actually means: pulses are seeds and foods simultaneously. They have been passed on from hand to hand, farmer to farmer, generation to generation for all that time. They have never stopped being alive or we wouldn't be growing them now.

THE YEAR OF PULSES: TOP FIVE PICKS

The year 2016 is designated the International Year of Pulses by the United Nations' Food and Agricultural Organization. The term "pulse" refers to legumes harvested primarily for the dry seed. This excludes green beans and green peas, both considered vegetables, and also omits clovers and alfalfa, which are mainly used as cover crops. Also not included are soybeans and peanuts, which have a much higher oil content. Pulses contain virtually no fat.

For this book, I have focused on the five pulse crops that grow best in North America and which I am the most familiar with. There are lots of other pulses—including lima, mung and tepary beans, cowpeas and pigeon peas—that prefer summers hotter than we have in most of Canada and the United States, including where I grow them on Salt Spring Island, British Columbia.

Although all pulses offer much to celebrate, dry peas and beans, chickpeas, favas and lentils really stand out for their amazing track record and ease of cultivation. They are *the* five most important pulse crops and feature

Opposite: Dried beans often come in very pretty packages—the Borlotti Bean has a startling pink colour.

prominently in the traditional cuisines of virtually every region of the globe.

Accelerated climate change has led to a lot of talk about saving our world. There seems to be a big upsurge of thinking and wondering if it could be possible. I'm writing this book to make my case for pulses being key to finding that answer.

What would happen if we dropped the kill-your-enemy syndrome we've got going now, the one we've always had on this planet, and replaced it with a "there are no enemies" approach? If everyone got together and thought about how we could all live peacefully with each other, wouldn't the starting point be how we are going to have enough food to eat and clean water for all? What a promising new beginning we would have if we actually figured that out!

Pulses are a protein-rich superfood that can be grown organically anywhere, using very little water *and* boosting soil wherever they take root. Delicious, versatile and easy to store, they are the perfect food for this planet and *all* its people.

To my mind, the pulse foods are waving at us beckoningly, saying, "You figured us out ten thousand years ago, you figured us out 8 thousand, 6 thousand, 4 thousand and 2 thousand years ago—and you're figuring us out now."

HEALTHY PULSES, HEALTHY PLANET

Pulses are actually coming on stronger than ever and are outstanding seeds for our future.[2] Canadian farmers are proclaiming that the Prairies, despite already being the world's largest pulse exporter, could grow enough pulses to feed another billion people. Galen Weston, the chief of Canada's largest food retailer, Loblaws, calls pulses "the food of the future" and key to keeping populations fed.[3] And, of course, the United Nations has given pulses its top honour and designated 2016 as the International Year of Pulses in recognition of the crucial role they can play in the future of our earth.[4]

Not only are pulses the best foods to weave together all the other foods we have to eat, they offer the potential to weave together a healthy planet for all.

But we can't keep on growing pulses with poisons and we can't continue to endorse an agriculture that relies on poisons. We have to stop swallowing the ludicrous propaganda that the foods we eat

The Purple-podded Pole Pea delights the eye before it delights the taste buds. *Carol Pope photo*

need herbicides and pesticides to be grown successfully. Pulses are healthiest without poisons. People are too.

I happened on a newspaper editorial that was trying to account for the alarming increases in stomach, gut and bowel problems in the North American population in the past few decades. It's no mystery to me (or to a lot of other people) why so many Canadians and Americans are so sick these days. I believe strongly that this is the result of herbicides such as glyphosate (more commonly known as Roundup) being in virtually everything we eat. From keen observation over a 30-year period, I'd say that the growth in these human health issues has paralleled agriculture's increasing use of poisons on "enemy" weeds and pests.

I believe that the residues of herbicides and pesticides disrupt and abort the very complex interactions that go on inside the human body and they can do so even in very minute doses. Thus I feel sure this is one of the key reasons for the huge upsurges over the last couple decades in celiac, Crohn's and Alzheimer's diseases, as well as many kinds of cancers.

THE POWER OF PULSES

I'm not the only one who feels strongly about this. Dr. Thierry Vrain, a retired genetic engineer and soil biologist with Agriculture Canada, made a cross-Canada tour to speak about engineered food and its impact on human health, presenting strong evidence to back up his concern that, due to the prevalence of "Roundup Ready" crops (crops engineered to withstand Roundup), "glyphosate is involved and mostly responsible for the epidemic of inflammatory and degenerative diseases that we have seen in the last 15 years."[5]

He also notes that "many pulse crops are now sprayed with a desiccant called Roundup WeatherMAX just before harvest if they are not completely dry or if there are weeds in the fields—like so many other crops that are not engineered (cereals, sunflower, sugar cane, etc.) because the combines prefer dry rather than green." Clearly, growing your own or sourcing organic food from local farmers is the best way to go for everything you eat.

Chemical warfare on plants and insects also destroys the complex biology of the soil. That's why food production continues to decrease on the huge acreages of monoculture farming.

In 2013, the United Nations Conference on Trade and Development published a document called *Wake Up Before It Is Too Late: Make Agriculture Truly Sustainable Now for Food Security in a Changing Climate*. The report includes contributions from more than 60 experts around the globe and concludes that small-scale organic farming is the only way to feed the world.[6] It stresses the immediate need to return agriculture to its roots, and urged "a rapid and significant shift from conventional, monoculture-based and high-external-input-dependent industrial production towards mosaics of sustainable, regenerative production systems that also considerably improve the productivity of small-scale farmers."[7]

On top of this, the United Nations declared 2015 the International Year of Soils.[8] Their intention was to highlight how essential a part "soil plays in food security, climate-change adaptation and mitigation, essential ecosytem services, poverty alleviation and sustainable development."

And now 2016 has been declared the UN International Year of Pulses. What better point in time for farmers and gardeners to embrace the need to transform our currently unsustainable agriculture model than by growing pulses? In fact, many organic farmers are learning that pulses are a vital part of healthy plant

Opposite: Like many pole beans, Celina's Pole Bean has long pods that are great fresh and also develop excellent dry beans. *Photo courtesy jatrax/Thinkstock*

rotation, building the soil and naturally strengthening all the crops so that they are more resistant to insect infestations and disease.[9]

Awareness has sprouted in North America among the many farmers who know how easily pulses grow here; they are presently cultivating and sending incredible amounts—millions of tonnes, worth billions of dollars—to 150-plus countries that know and value pulses highly.[10] The next step, surely, is for us to be *eating* our own pulses as well as growing them *without* those unnecessary destructive and dangerous inputs.

FOOD SECURITY, SEED SECURITY

With such rapid and radical climate change occurring, food security has never before been so cogent an issue. Pulses stand out for their nutrition, yields, hardiness and adaptability. Food security also comes from seed security, because you can't grow good food without good seed.

Unlike many foods—such as carrots, beets, broccoli and kale—pulses are the food you eat plus the seed for next year's crop. You don't have to overwinter pulses in the garden and there are no special seed-saving procedures. Aside from a minor exception in the case of favas, there is nothing to worry about in terms of keeping varieties true. So farmers and gardeners can be both bean growers and seed savers without additional work or infrastructure.

SMALLER FARMS, BIGGER YIELDS

At present, the average North American farm is more than 500 acres (200 hectares)[11] and fewer than 2 percent of the people in North America are farmers.[12] With farms that big, it's almost impossible to manage everything without gigantic machinery, huge chemical inputs and a total disconnection from nature. On 5 to 20 acre (2 to 8 hectare) farms, many people could be joyfully and healthfully occupied in growing the best quality foods without poisons. Hands would actually touch the earth and lungs would take in fresh air. A group of 10 people could mulch an acre of beans by hand in a day.

Peasant farmers would have a lot to show us about sustainable farming if we dropped our arrogance long enough to listen. The agriculture that has been a disaster for people and the land, that same agriculture that we've been trying to impose on all the rest

of the world, is still not the predominant model worldwide. In fact, 95 percent of the world's farms are less than 12 acres (5 hectares) and more than 2 billion people depend on small farms for their livelihoods. Small-scale farmers produce 70 percent of the world's food on just 25 percent of the world's farmland. And, according to USC Canada, switching from conventional to sustainable methods can see a rise in crop yields of up to 79 percent.[13]

More and more gardens could also complement smaller farms and boost pulse power big-time. The Victory Gardens that were created around home gardens and public parks during the first and second world wars show what can be achieved with smaller-scale food growing. Also called "food gardens for defense," they became an important part of daily life on the home front, boosted civil morale and helped the war effort by taking over a major part of food production. In World War II, more than eighteen million Victory Gardens grew a third of US vegetable production. (That's when the bland white navy beans mentioned later in this book— as the beans *not* to grow!—had their heyday.)

Unknown to most North Americans, there is a country right now admirably demonstrating that small-scale organic gardening can indeed feed the world. That nation is Russia, where self-sufficiency in food is a government priority. On a total of about 20 million acres, 16.5 million families grow food in small-scale organic gardens on their *dachas*. These are seasonal or year-round second homes that are subsidized by the government:

There can be over 250 pods on a single chickpea plant. *Karen Mouat photo*

Each chickpea pod has one or two chickpeas.
Karen Mouat photo

An impressive 40 percent of Russia's total agricultural output comes from these dacha gardens, including almost 80 percent of potatoes, 66 percent of vegetables and more than 80 percent of fruits and berries, along with half the nation's milk.[14]

There is a very short growing season in most of Russia, so imagine what could be done in Canada, or in the United States, where, at present, lawns take up more than twice the amount of land Russia's gardens do.[15]

SUMMER CROPS, WINTER CROPS

Peas, chickpeas, favas and lentils can be grown in winter where it is mild and summers where it's not too hot. They are all winter crops in the Mediterranean and could easily thrive in the cooler seasons of much of the southern United States.

Beans, on the other hand, are pretty much a summer crop everywhere. With the many short-season varieties available, anyone blessed with a sunny site can have a crop that dries to perfection in the garden.

SLOW FOOD, FAST FOOD

Slow Food is an international movement, founded in 1989, that strives to preserve traditional and regional cuisine. The culinary enjoyment of pulses would certainly be included as a slow-food activity.

Fast food is what many, if not most, people in North America eat every single day because they haven't the time or place to cook their own food. It's what you get from the fast-food outlets, as well as all the processed, packaged products you find in supermarkets.

Virtually all fast foods contain genetically modified organisms (GMOs), because most of their ingredients are derivatives of GMO corn (for the syrup) and GMO soybeans (for the protein).[16] In two short decades, GMO corn and soybean cultivation has gone from test plots to the point of making up most of the yield of commercial cultivated acreage.[17]

GMO crops are genetically engineered to withstand applications of Roundup so you're very likely to be eating glyphosate herbicide when you're eating your fast food. As I've noted, Roundup is a powerful poison, even in minute amounts—not only does it destroy important internal biological processes, it also depletes food of essential mineral micronutrients.[18] The more fast foods you eat, the less you are nourished and the more you crave food.

Here is another way that pulses could save the world. Ecologically grown peas and beans, chickpeas, favas and lentils could be used to make fast foods that are healthy instead of deadly. The excellent nutritional profile of pulses could be utilized with other organically grown food to make breads, crackers, chips, spreads, pasta and burgers. There are some excellent processed pulse products already and it's strikingly clear that one of the best slow foods around has the potential to take over the fast-food market.

THE NEED FOR PULSES

As I write this in the summer of 2015, the Canadian Gulf Islands, where I live, are in the midst of unprecedented heat and drought. Serious restrictions on water usage are in effect and many people are watching their gardens wither and die. At the same time, hundreds of fires are burning across western Canada and the United States, with thousands of people having to leave their homes.

It is likely that everyone reading this has her or his own local story of floods or fires, excessive heat or cold. We are indeed in the midst of accelerated climate change.

New research supported by the United Kingdom's Foreign and Commonwealth Office[19] and insurer Lloyd's of London[20] warns of imminent catastrophic food shortages due to unchecked climate change. Last year, the UN's Intergovernmental Panel on Climate Change similarly asserted that humanity is risking a "breakdown of food systems linked to warming, drought, flooding, and precipitation variability and extremes"[21] on its current path of unrestricted carbon pollution.

The time to act strongly and swiftly is now. In our concern about how agriculture is threatened by climate change, we mustn't lose sight of the fact that it is our present mode of growing food that is helping to create such radical weather variations.

It is estimated that the global food system is responsible for a full third of the world's total greenhouse gas emissions. According to the UN's Food and Agricultural Organization, livestock production alone contributes about 18 percent of the global warming effect—more than the emissions from every single car, train and plane on the planet.

An excellent book about food and climate change is *Diet for a Hot Planet* by Anna Lappé. With much scientific backup, the author makes it powerfully clear that our fossil-fuelled industrialized food system is wreaking havoc on us all.

We must get deadly serious now about the question of how to feed ourselves so that our grandchildren will be able to feed themselves and so will their grandchildren. Here's to the power of pulses!

THE GIFT OF PULSES

For 30 years, I've watched pulses improve the fertility of my soils by simply growing. I've seen how sun, soil life and pulse plants work together so that, when I sow a bean in the same spot the following year, the new plant grows even more vigorously than

its predecessor. And the next will be even more productive. And so it goes.

For 30 years, I have grown my pulse crops with only the rare watering, mulching early on and then just standing back to watch them grow and produce food. It takes a huge amount of water to create everyday products—the T-shirt I'm wearing, for example, required 3,000 litres of water to grow and process the cotton. Pulses, on the other hand, can be cultivated—and usually are, even in large-scale production—without irrigation. That we can grow such a high-quality food without water and actually strengthen the earth at the same time is truly miraculous.

I believe pulse power is already an unstoppable force that is coming on stronger than ever. In the next few decades, pulses will increasingly replace steaks and cheese in the major meat- and dairy-consuming nations of the world.

While peas, beans, chickpeas, favas and lentils aren't the only power foods—there are so many fruits, nuts, berries, seeds and

The Blooming Prairie bean is a visual delight that can be snacked right in the garden. Named for a town in Minnesota, it is a fine dried bean and also delicious when steamed fresh. *Karen Mouat photo*

THE POWER OF PULSES

greens that can all contribute to a rich and diverse diet—they are the best all-around for ease of growing, nutrition and ecological sustainability. When I started Salt Spring Seeds in 1986, I listed only 10 cultivars in my single-page catalogue, 9 of which were beans. Now I have over 700 types of food seeds in my online catalogue, including 80 hardy and prolific varieties of pulses.

Since the beginning, my Salt Spring Seeds motto has been "Dedicated to a Safe and Sustainable Agriculture." Now I'm thinking that "safe" and "sustainable"—though good words—don't convey enough.

True, humans have been growing food without poisoning themselves for 9,950 of the last 10,000 years, so there is every reason to pursue safe farming with every confidence. And "sustainable" also speaks to the notion of our going on and on. Pulses, however, point to the possibility of going onwards and upwards. With their wonderful soil associations, they remind us that we, too, exist in relationships—that myriad life forms are present all around us, on us and even inside of us for mutual benefit. Peas, beans, chickpeas, favas and lentils have the power to keep making our relationship to the earth better and better. Not only can they sustain us, they can also renew us.

The power of pulses is that they feed us with the knowledge that we don't have to be all-powerful: there is not only enough, but more than enough, for everyone.

Opposite: Fresh green beans in summer—what a treat! (*Christina Symons photo*). *Above left:* The many different kinds of pulses are often simply called beans (*Photo courtesy alisafarov/ Thinkstock*). *Above right:* Chickpeas can be shelled while still green and eaten like shelling peas. They are sweet and nutty (*Photo © Jan Mangan*).

Growing beans on trellises or fencing gives you high productivity per planting row. *Karen Mouat photo*

SIX STRATEGIES FOR EMPOWERING PULSES

Wider recognition of the bounty and beauty of pulses is, no doubt, on its way. The designation of 2016 by the United Nations as the International Year of Pulses creates unprecedented opportunity for pulses to be recognized for the rich and replenishing resource they are. The truth of pulse power will radiate as never before when people realize how brilliantly pulses can help nourish and heal the planet.

We can help that process along in a few easy ways.

1. As gardeners, we can grow peas and beans, chickpeas, favas and lentils. They are easier to grow and more rewarding than just about any other garden crop and we can all discover the best varieties for our own growing situation.

    Although garden seed catalogues rarely offer any pulses besides regular beans, I can mention a few excellent sources for most of the pulses. They are all friends and like-minded pulse advocates who have small mail-order seed companies:

- Jim and Rachelle Ternier's Prairie Garden Seeds (Humboldt, SK)
- Krista Rome's Backyard Beans & Grains Project (Everson, WA)
- Owen Bridge's Annapolis Seeds (Middleton, NS)
- And my own seed company, Salt Spring Seeds, always stands behind pulses

2. Another option for obtaining seeds to plant is found in the bulk dry foods section in supermarkets and health food stores. Customers of mine are always surprised when I tell them they can purchase a pound of organic lentils or chickpeas for a couple of dollars from their local store instead of buying a few ounces from me for $3.50 plus postage. Some stores offer quite a few choices. If the seeds are organic, they should be viable for growing.

3. As consumers, we can encourage store managers to stock whole dry organic pulses as well as pulse products. We can stress the importance of trying to obtain these as locally as possible. There are also exciting possibilities for featuring pulse recipes in grocery-store delicatessens and for highlighting the farmers who grew them.

4. Pulse dishes in restaurants are often the cheapest, most delicious items on the menu—order them as often as you can!

5. We can also support and encourage all suppliers of fresh local beans, peas, chickpeas, favas and lentils by buying their pulses whenever possible and telling them that we appreciate what they do.

6. And, as gardeners, consumers, farmers and cooks, we can commit ourselves, as eaters, to take the time to cook, enjoy and celebrate pulses.

CHAPTER 2

Pulse Power
FOR BETTER HEALTH

The fact that pulses have been the mainstay of diets in many countries for thousands of years speaks volumes about their nutrition and versatility. If you research the nutritional components of peas, beans, chickpeas, favas and lentils, it is shiningly clear what nourishing foods they are.

According to health experts, pulses are a superfood: eating pulses may help to prevent several cancers (including breast, colon and prostate), lower cholesterol, control blood glucose levels, optimize blood pressure, reduce heart and peripheral artery disease and promote gut health and liver function.[22] Research points to pulses also helping to strengthen bones to prevent breakage, boost cognitive abilities and sharpen memory, and reduce oxidative stress and inflammation in the body. Rich in protein and high in vitamin B, pulses are an excellent food for vegetarians and vegans. Gluten-free and full of protein, pulses are also very beneficial for those with celiac disease or any type of gluten intolerance.[23]

Examine practically any nutritional label on purchased food items and you'll rarely find protein, mineral and vitamin contents above a small percentage per serving. On the other hand, the nutritional value per daily serving of any of the pulses is usually 30 percent of the recommended daily amounts for most nutrients.

Opposite: Pulses come in a stunning variety of colours.

NUTRITION FULL, PROTEIN RICH

Pulses are 20 to 30 percent protein by weight. Eating pulses with grains, nuts or seeds ensures a high-quality complete protein. To learn more about this, read one or all of these great books:

- *Diet for a New America: How Your Food Choices Affect Your Health, Happiness and the Future of Life on Earth*, by John Robbins
- *Diet for a Small Planet*, by Frances Moore Lappé
- *High Steaks: Why and How to Eat Less Meat*, by Eleanor Boyle
- *Diet for a Hot Planet: The Climate Crisis at the End of Your Fork and What You Can Do about It*, by Anna Lappé

HIGH FIBRE, LOW CHOLESTEROL

Pulses are very high in fibre, containing both soluble and insoluble fibre. Regular consumption of pulses helps lower cholesterol and other blood lipid levels,[24] while insoluble fibre helps with digestion and maintaining regular bowel movements. There is much evidence that high-fibre diets reduce the risk of certain

Opposite: Most beans are delicious with little adornment (*Christina Symons photo*). *Above:* Beans darkening to purple as they dry down (*Karen Mouat photo*).

Above: Pulses can be featured in a wide variety of recipes, including Red Lentil Condiment, recipe on page 122 (Christina Symons photos). Opposite: Shelled favas ready for steaming (Photo courtesy violleta/ Thinkstock).

cancers. Fibre-rich foods like pulses are often more satisfying than other foods, helping you keep full until your next meal, an added bonus for those watching their weight.

LOW GLYCEMIC INDEX, GOOD ENERGY

Pulses have a low glycemic index.[25] Most of the carbohydrates in pulses prevent blood sugars from rising quickly after a meal or snack. Eating foods with a low glycemic index can help you to control your blood glucose levels, maintain high energy levels throughout the day, control your appetite and lower your risk of developing type 2 diabetes.

LIGHT ON FAT, HEART HEALTHY

Pulses are very low in fat and sodium and they are free of trans fats and cholesterol, making them an extremely heart-healthy option. In contrast to other protein sources such as meat and cheese, pulses contain virtually no fat.[26]

B VITAMINS, HEALTHY CELLS

Pulses are an excellent source of folate, a B vitamin shown to lower homocysteine levels. Evidence suggests that high levels of homocysteine (a type of protein) can damage the lining of arteries and cause plaque buildup and blood clots, both of which can impede blood flow to the heart or brain, causing a heart attack or stroke. Folate also plays an important role in cell development,

and is particularly important during infancy and pregnancy when new cells are rapidly developing.[27]

Pulses are a good source of other B vitamins too, such as thiamin (B_1), riboflavin (B_2), niacin (B_3), pantothenic acid (B_5) and pyridoxine (B_6), essential for healthy cells and deriving energy from the food we eat.

GLUTEN-FREE, VERSATILE IN THE KITCHEN

Pulses make ideal gluten-free flour for breads, pancakes, cakes, muffins, cookies and thickeners for soups and sauces. While there are other gluten-free flours available, including potato and rice, these can leave diets short on protein, fibre and B vitamins. Gluten-free pulse flours, on the other hand, include slowly digestible carbohydrates[28] and are rich in protein, fibre, iron and particularly in B vitamins.[29] Mixing pulse flour with brown rice flour or another gluten-free grain, such as amaranth, provides a complete and delicious protein.[30]

When replacing wheat flour with pulse flour in any recipe for baked goods, add xanthan gum or guar gum to perform the function of gluten and ensure the result is not crumbly. For low-rise cookies, ¼ tsp (1 mL) per cup (250 mL) of flour is enough. For cakes, go to ½ tsp (2.5 mL), for muffins and quick breads ¾ tsp (4 mL), and for breads and pizza 1 to 1½ tsp (5 to 7.5 mL).

Pulse flour is denser and more flavourful than rice or potato flours, so foods made from it are more substantial and satisfying. And in addition to having a pleasing, solid and slightly moist texture, baked goods also taste better! See Dan's Gluten-free Honey and Spice Bean Bread, page 175.

Opposite: Yellow wax beans can be snacked fresh or steamed for a few minutes.

Pulse flours absorb more moisture than other flours, so you may need to increase the liquid slightly when making baked goods.

Socca, a flatbread made from chickpea flour, is one of many possibilities for delicious gluten-free baked goods made from pulse flours (recipe on page 113).

GRINDING GLUTEN-FREE FLOUR FROM PULSES

You can grind your own flour from pulses using a blender or flour mill. (But do crack larger pulses open in the blender first before grinding in a mill.) If there are any hard bits that don't break down into a fine flour, sift them out and pulverize them in a coffee or spice grinder 1 to 2 Tbsp (15 to 30 mL) at a time.

Each pulse offers a slightly different texture and flavour of flour. Choose from chickpeas, lentils or small beans. You can also experiment with roasting your pulses first—no more than 20 minutes at 350F (180C)—to ease the grinding and give your flour a nuttier flavour. Or roast the flour itself in the oven in an uncovered cast iron frying pan for a similar amount of time to enrich its flavour, stirring with a fork every 3 to 4 minutes so that it browns evenly.

After grinding, store your pulse flour in an airtight container in a cool and dry place, or freeze to keep it super-fresh.

Pulse flours are often available in supermarkets, health food stores and Indian, Middle Eastern and Asian food stores. Chickpea flour (also called *besan* or *gram* flour) is by far the most popular and easiest to find.

HIGH IN POTASSIUM, MINERAL RICH

Pulses are high in potassium, a mineral that helps regulate fluid balance and maintain normal blood pressure, and are a good source of other important minerals such as iron, zinc, magnesium[31] and calcium.[32]

POUND OF PULSES, OUNCE OF PREVENTION

World Health Organization studies show that roughly 80 percent of heart disease, strokes and type 2 diabetes, along with a third of all cancers, are the result of unnecessary risk factors including an unhealthy diet. Notably high in fibre, minerals and B vitamins, pulses are strongly recommended as a part of any diet to encourage good health and longevity.[33] In a prominent study, it was shown that eating a little less than 1 ounce (30 g) of legumes a day led on average to a 7 to 8 percent reduction in mortality among similar candidates.[34]

That all makes for a lot of power in a pound of pulses, yet they'll be about the cheapest food in the store. And if you're growing your own, you'll be rewarded beyond measure!

THE FLATULENCE FACTOR: EASY TO AVOID

People who have never before tried homegrown dry peas and beans, chickpeas, favas and lentils are surprised and very pleased by the absence of "the flatulence factor."

Yes, here's an important secret: if pulses are eaten within a year of harvest, they won't give you gas! The sad truth is that most pulses you buy have travelled thousands of miles and were picked years ago. Like all perishable food, they age and oxidize; they just do it a little more slowly so it's not as noticeable. They become less digestible as time goes on.

Most cultures have never had this problem with pulses because they keep growing them and don't eat old seeds. Our own industrial agriculture is about supply and demand and not about keeping "fresh" dry beans in the marketplace.

It's always a thrill for me to see my freshly harvested pulses on my drying screens just before putting them away—not only are the colours and patterns diverse and beautiful, each variety has a radiant shine that is hard to describe. You don't usually find this glow with store-bought pulses. In fact, when you get to observe how your own beans get duller and darker with age, you get an idea of how very old the ones in your health food store can be.

Besides eating your own homegrown, there are other ways to minimize the flatulence factor that are very effective when using store-bought pulses:

1. Presoak and change the soaking water two to three times, replenishing the pot with fresh water each time, to wash away carbohydrates that can cause gas.
2. Rinse pulses well after they have been soaked.
3. As uncooked starch is hard to digest, ensure your pulses are adequately cooked (see Pulse Soaking and Cooking Times, page 101).

In my experience, two "solutions" that are often recommended—adding salt or baking soda—do not work. Salt can harden pulses and slow down the cooking process. In addition to possibly making your pulses too soft, baking soda destroys thiamin, an important B vitamin.

Opposite: Amish Snap Pea. Most pea flowers are white but they also come in combinations of pink and purple.

CHAPTER 3

Growing
YOUR OWN PULSES

Peas, chickpeas, favas and lentils are sown in early spring. Warm-weather beans are planted in late spring. Sunny exposures are more important for beans, chickpeas and lentils than for favas and peas, which prefer a cooler position in the garden.

Some people like to soak their pulses overnight in cold water before planting. This will speed things up if the soil is relatively warm but isn't recommended if the seeds are going into cold ground. I usually don't bother with this, as it only makes a difference of a day or two and often results in cracked seed and more difficult sowing; however, it can help speed things along if you are getting a late-season start on planting.

NITROGEN NODULES, BACTERIA BOOSTERS

When planting any pulse variety for the first time, it can be helpful, though not crucial, to coat the seeds with a specific bacterial inoculant to jumpstart the process of nitrogen-fixing.

The inoculant is a fine powder composed of beneficial *Rhizobium* bacteria that congregate to create swollen nodes at points along the pea roots. These nodules draw nitrogen from the air and convert it to make the nitrogen accessible to plants, which helps them grow and increases the fertility of the soil for future crops. In return, the legume crops provide these friendly bacteria with a source of carbon produced by photosynthesis.

Opposite: These King Tut Soup Peas are on their way to drying down. *Photo © Jan Mangan*

Specific bacteria work with peas, beans, chickpeas, favas and lentils, so it's important to source the particular inoculant for each of these crops. The inoculants don't have specialized names—they are just called "pea inoculant," "bean inoculant," etc., and are available at some garden shops or through seed companies.

Pulses are inherently adept at creating their own nitrogen-fixing arrangements—once these bacteria are in the soil, they multiply rapidly and persist indefinitely—so inoculants are mostly helpful in the first year. If you don't have the appropriate inoculant, that doesn't need to stop you from planting pulses in that first year; while adding inoculant is helpful, it is certainly not essential.

Spacing Your Pulse Plants

I space my pulse rows about 18 inches (46 cm) apart. This distance makes it easy to walk the rows and mulch the plants. As well, it keeps the plants from becoming too congested. The spacing within the rows for each crop varies, as do height and support requirements:

Peas	2 inches (5 cm) apart
Beans	6–8 inches (15–20 cm) apart
Chickpeas	12 inches (30 cm) apart
Favas	10 inches (25 cm) apart
Lentils	6 inches (15 cm) apart

FERTILE GROUND, FINDING THE RIGHT BALANCE

While pulses thrive in moderately rich ground, they also do well in a wide range of soils, even without amendments. In especially acidic soil, the addition of bone meal, wood ash, dolomite lime or compost will moderate the acidity.

Earth with too much nitrogen will promote excessive leaf growth and delay and reduce pod production. Hold back on adding nitrogen, but don't be afraid to keep planting pulses—I've been growing them for years and the soil continues to be optimal for growing all crops. While you can push your soil's nitrogen content higher than is optimal with the addition of too much manure or fertilizer, you won't get out of balance with too much nitrogen by planting pulses year after year.

Opposite: Open-ended greenhouses can enable an early planting and an early harvest for pulses. Plus, they erase all worries about rain soaking mature beans.
Photo © Jan Mangan

Schweizer Riesen Pea
flowers. *Carol Pope photo*

EASY TO PLANT, QUICK TO GROW

As a rule of thumb, pulses are planted to a depth similar to their
length. That is, if the seed is an inch (2.5 cm) long, it should be
sown so that it is covered by an inch of soil. It is best to plant
within a few days of working the ground so that the soil surface
is still relatively moist and loose. If planting after some days of
hot sun, plant a little deeper so there is moisture for the seeds to
absorb, and/or give the soil a good watering.

Most other seeds, such as those for greens, roots and herbs, are
much smaller than beans and there is danger of them sprouting
only to die if dry weather lasts for many days. Pulses have much
more holding power because of their size and ability to absorb
considerable water. You can almost always trust pulses to successfully germinate within seven to ten days and to captivate you as
they thrust into the light.

WATER LESS, MULCH MORE

As already stated, all the pulses are very drought-tolerant crops. Once they are on their way and growing leaves, you shouldn't need to water them.

Mulching makes doubly sure you won't need to water and is a practice that works especially well with pulses. The best mulch materials are leaves or straw (essentially the bare stalks left after grain heads have been harvested). Hay (grain with the heads) containing weed seeds is also fine if you know that those seeds are relatively innocuous (not the likes of thistle or burdock seeds). The goal is to mulch thickly enough that weeds can't get started. So don't leave any bare ground exposed and mulch densely enough that there is no space for weeds to get through. Wait until the plants are firmly established and 3 to 5 inches (7.5 to 13 cm) high—you can mulch right up to the stalk.

Mulching prevents crusting of the soil surface and results in a light, fluffy and porous soil that enhances root development and effective drainage. It also provides a protective surface for unsupported plants to sprawl on and keeps them mud-free and drier, reducing the chance of mildew, mould, rust and blight.

Mulching saves a lot of time and energy in the long run. It preserves intricate earthworm tunnels and eliminates the need for

Pulse Plant Heights

While it's best to provide trellising or teepees made with stakes for climbing peas and beans to cling to, all other pulses are self-supporting. In windy locations, though, you may want to provide favas with a bit of a buffer by staking each end of the row and enclosing the plants with string.

Peas	Bush 2–3 feet (60–90 cm); climbing can reach 7 feet (2 m) (support required)
Beans	Bush 18–60 inches (46–150 cm); climbing can reach 8 feet (244 cm) (support required)
Chickpeas	8–20 inches (20–50 cm)
Favas	20–70 inches (50–180 cm) (require support only in windy locations)
Lentils	15–18 inches (40–46 cm)

Use weighted down mesh planting trays (left) or start seedlings in pots (right) to protect your newly planted pulses from ravenous birds. *Carol Pope photos*

most hoeing and weeding. Weeds that do poke through the mulch are weakly rooted and easy to pull, or may be mulched over again. After harvest the mulch can be left on the soil to be dug into the ground in spring.

I mulch all the pulses I grow. Combined with the nitrogen-fixing ability of pulses, mulching improves the soil very noticeably each year. The only time I hold back on mulch is early in spring when mulching would keep the soil cooler than if directly exposed to sunlight.

HUNGRY BIRDS AND PESTS

The only serious problem I've had with growing pulses over the years has been with birds eating them once they are planted. If birds notice any of the pulses sprouting out of the ground, they will feast on them. To prevent this, I almost always mulch my pea rows with straw or hay right after planting. Unlike the other pulses, peas can sprout well through mulch. That usually works, although I have also heard quite a few stories of mice eating freshly planted peas, even if camouflaged with mulch.

Another solution is growing your pulses in containers and transplanting them after a few weeks of growth. This works well, although you may still have problems with mice or birds unless you place your seeded pots in a sheltered location or give them some protection. Covering a tray of potted seedlings with an overturned plastic mesh planting tray that still lets in rain and

sunshine is a reliable solution, provided you place two fist-sized rocks on top to keep nosy foragers out.

Or, if you prefer to protect your seedlings one pot at a time, you can place an upside-down mesh strawberry basket over each pot, again with a stone set firmly on top.

You can also use this strategy to direct-sow. Simply plant into the ground and then place overturned mesh planting trays or strawberry baskets over the seedlings and secure with sturdy rocks.

When the first set of mature leaves begins to develop (and is likely just starting to press against the ceiling of the mesh tray or basket), go ahead and pull away your protective measures. The pulse has grown past the point of being bird or rodent food now and is ready to reach for the sky!

Another pulse-planting strategy for those with a protected planting space that has good light is to use a section of guttering for planting. Simply fill a piece of guttering with potting soil and plant as you would in the garden, thinning as necessary. When the pulses have developed their first set of mature leaves, dig a trough

You can also use planting trays to protect potted pulse seeds from predators. *Carol Pope photo*

Old pieces of guttering can make great do-it-yourself pea planters. *Carol Pope photo*

out in the garden similar in depth to the guttering and gently slide the plantings into it. Snug them into place with soil wherever necessary. This involves a minimum of fussing and allows your pulses to germinate in a protected spot safe from hungry birds and rodents.

I can't speak much to pests and diseases, having only experienced the occasional aphid. Aphids can be sprayed off with a hose and heavily infested leaves can be pinched off, provided you don't defoliate the plant too drastically. Or, if you are patient, ants usually show up to farm the aphids, a process that is fascinating to watch. I've heard from friends with bean beetle problems that picking off the beetles by hand is successful, though tedious.

Another strategy for supporting organic growing is to add plants that attract pest-gobbling beneficial insects to your garden. Ladybugs, for example, will flock to plants like yarrow, cornflower, alyssum and lovage. And the lacewing, another avid aphid eater, loves borage, along with fennel and other plants from the carrot

family. Aromatic herbs as companion plants help too—rosemary, for example, is known to repel those bean beetles.

There are a few precautions worth mentioning to ensure healthy organic harvests:

- Don't risk spreading rusts, mildews or blights by working among wet plants.
- Remove or turn under plant debris when the plants are finished.
- Rotate your crops if you notice any problems; you should do this routinely every three years or so either way.
- Plant a diversity of crops so that diseases or pests are held in check.
- Add plants that attract beneficial insects that eat garden pests.
- Space your crops (see page 30) to allow good circulation between them.
- Mulch to keep weeds at bay and preserve moisture in the soil, ensuring more robust, disease- and pest-resistant crops.

Plant rosemary near your bean plants to help discourage bean beetles.
Carol Pope photo

Threshing bean pods in a wooden box takes only 2 to 3 minutes. For small quantities, a plastic tub works just as well. *Karen Mouat photos*

HARVEST TIME, PICK WHILE DRY

For all the pulses, it is optimum to let the pods dry on the plant. If extended wet weather threatens, pods that are nearly dry and brittle can be picked to finish drying under cover. In the case of lentils, entire plants are best cut at the base because it would be too time-consuming to pick all the pods.

Pulses are ready when a fingernail can't make an indentation in the seed. Once harvested, your pulses should be spread out to dry in their pods.

DRYING PODS, THRESHING PULSES

Don't open pods to let your pulses dry or the natural drying process will be aborted; let them dry inside unopened pods.

Your pulse harvest should be laid out on screens or cookie cooling racks in a protected, well-ventilated space for a few days until you are certain that every last seed is stone dry. Inspect them for bugs and signs of damage and discard all suspect seeds.

Once dry, it is easy to open regular bean, pea and fava pods by hand but quite difficult to do so with chickpeas and lentils. All the pulses can easily be threshed by foot in a good-sized tub or wooden box. I use what I call my threshing box, which is simply a 2 × 3-foot (60 × 90-cm) wooden box that has sides about 18 inches (46 cm) high and thin wooden slats on the bottom for extra abrasion. Walking on the brittle pods inside the box and rubbing them against the slats releases the seeds in just a few minutes. Lentils are best threshed plant and all.

Pulse Garden Harvests

You can expect high yields from all the pulses with the exception of lentils. Just three or four plants of peas, beans, chickpeas or favas will provide enough for a good meal for a family of four. With lentils, you'd need half a dozen plants.

Peas	10 feet (3 m) of climbing peas: more than 4 pounds (1.8 kg)
	20 feet (6 m) of bush peas: 4 pounds (1.8 kg)
Beans	10 feet (3 m) of climbing beans: more than 4 pounds (1.8 kg)
	20 feet (6 m) of bush beans: 4 pounds (1.8 kg)
Chickpeas	20 feet (6 m): 4–6 pounds (1.8–2.7 kg)
Favas	10 feet (3 m): more than 4 pounds (1.8 kg)
Lentils	20 feet (6 m): 2 pounds (0.9 kg)

If shucked by hand, the pods and seeds are nicely separated. Otherwise, the pod debris from stomping can be sifted out using screens or blown away with the nozzle attachment of an air compressor or a small fan or blow-dryer.

THE COLOUR AND COMPLEXITY OF PULSES

While pulse crops have their similarities, they also have many differences that make them a beautiful addition to the garden and the kitchen.

ROUND OR BLOCKY

Peas can be round or blocky. Small favas can look like large peas, while large favas can look like oversized kidney beans. Chickpeas resemble peas with the added addition of a little protuberance at the sprouting end. Lentils (*Lens culinaris*) all have lens-shaped seeds. Regular beans can be round, blocky or elongated.

BLACK AND WHITE, DARK AND LIGHT

Pulses come in practically every colour. Many of the regular cooking beans have gorgeous patterns such as the black-and-white Orca or the burgundy-and-mustard Tiger Eye.

Opposite top: Freshly tilled valley bottom at Seed Spirit Farm (Chris Thoreau photo). Bottom left: Hanging out in the bean patch (Christina Symons photo). Bottom right: Someone should eat these snow peas soon or they will become soup peas! (Chris Thoreau photo). Next page: Karen Mouat photos

FRIESE WOODBOON

KLEIN SOLDATENBOON

RÔNER ROSSE

UGANDAN JADE BEAN

GIELE WALDEANTSJES

NEZ PERCE

BANTU from UGANDA
BEAN APR 29

WHITE RUNNER BEAN

SHIROLUSTRUCZ KOVINA

READE KROBBE

WIERINGER BOONTJE

PEARL SOUP PEA

CERISE DU JAPON

LEKATT
(WIERINGER x APPALOOSA)

CHAPTER 4

Dry Peas

To my mind, dry peas *(Pisum sativum)* are one of the most undervalued and underappreciated crops in North America. Not long ago, I was giving a talk in Calgary, Alberta, and the kind woman who drove me to the airport told me she had been searching much of the day in a number of supermarkets for whole dry peas to make a pea soup. She couldn't find any.

Consider that three-quarters of a million acres of dry peas are grown annually in Alberta.[35] Saskatchewan grows even more than this.[36] These are exported to countries like China, India and Bangladesh, while Canadians eat less than 1 percent of what is grown in their own country.

The two principal growing regions in the United States are the Northern Plains, comprised of Montana, Wyoming, North Dakota and South Dakota, and the Palouse, which includes southeastern Washington, northern Idaho and northeastern Oregon. Like Canadians, Americans consume very few of their own pulses.

Consider that North American farmers of dry peas sell three or four main varieties and that these are grown with herbicides and pesticides. Yet, for thousands of years, farmers having been growing many beautiful varieties of dry peas without poisons, simply by hand-weeding, hoeing, mulching and rotating crops.

And that's what I've been doing for the past 30 years—growing a multitude of peas without ever having to kill anything in my garden. New

Opposite, clockwise from top left: Swedish Red Pea, Amish Snap Pea, Carlin Pea, Blue Pod Desiree Pea, Gold Harvest Pea.

varieties of peas keep surprising me. Currently I list about 20 diverse cultivars in my online Salt Spring Seeds catalogue, and I keep discovering more.

Although many pea cultivars have been lost because of the narrow focus of industrial agriculture, there are still hundreds of pea varieties under cultivation by peasant farmers. I say it's time for more seed companies and farmers to begin to trial these in North America to find the most adaptable and hardy cultivars (especially those that don't rely on poisons for success!) and to embrace their diverse and rich potential.

PEAS THROUGH THE AGES

Peas have a long and illustrious history. Evidence of pea consumption goes back to 9750 BC, near present-day Burma and Tibet. An archaeological dig in northern Iraq dated pea consumption there to 7000 BC and in Switzerland and Hungary to over 5,000 years ago.

An Ancient Pea Dish

Greeks and Romans cultivated dry peas from about 500 BC. Apicius's famous *Cookery and Dining in Imperial Rome* contains dry pea recipes such as this one:

"Cook the peas, when skimmed, lay leeks, coriander and cumin on top. Crush pepper, lovage, cumin, dill and green basilica, wine and broth to taste, make it boil; when done stir well, put in what perchance should be missing and serve."

Farmers in China started growing peas around the 7th century and the French ruler Charlemagne planted peas in his grand gardens around AD 800. They became a staple food in Europe, the Middle East and North Africa during the Middle Ages.

In the 1600s, dry peas became popular in New France and the French Canadian pea soup was born. Voyageurs took peas with them as they explored the continent.

It wasn't until the 18th century that fresh garden peas started to become popular, but peas for drying still predominated and were celebrated. In 1850, an impressive book by Werner Dressendörfer

called *Vilmorin: The Vegetable Garden* had 50 pages devoted to the different varieties of cultivated peas for drying. The book lists 74 main pea cultivars and 120 less-important ones; the length and breadth of the descriptions far surpasses those found in any catalogue of peas available today.

Planting 10 feet (3m) of climbing peas can yield over 4 pounds (1.8 kg) of dried peas. *Chris Thoreau photo*

SOUP PEAS, STEWING PEAS

More than a thousand varieties of peas are in existence today, the greatest diversity being found in India, where they continue to be a major and essential part of the diet over the entire subcontinent.

The selection of heirloom peas I grow and offer through Salt Spring Seeds is a testament to their usage around the world and includes varieties such as Dutch Kapucijner, Swedish Red Pea, China Snow Pea, Amish Snap Pea, Brazilian Snack Pea, Carouby de Maussane Snow Pea, Japanese Climbing Snow Pea, King Tut Soup Pea and Russian Sugar Pea. All of these are fine soup and stewing peas, each with a slightly different taste and texture.

SWEDISH
RED PEA

*Above: Swedish Red Peas
are a rare claret colour.
They are a wonderful
cooking pea (Karen
Mouat photo). Opposite:
Japanese Climbing Snow
Pea pods (Photo © Jan
Mangan).*

DRY PEAS VS. FRESH

Many people have asked me if fresh shelling peas make good
dry peas if you let them dry on the vine. The answer is no.

Shelling peas, such as Alderman (Tall Telephone) and Green
Arrow, have been bred to be sugary sweet when you pop them
fresh out of the pod into your mouth. When they dry down they
don't have as rich a taste or as pleasant a texture as traditional
soup and stewing peas, nor do they have the same level of nutrition as peas grown for drying.

Instead of drying shelling peas, you can freeze them to add to
soups and stir-fries for winter meals.

EDIBLE POD PEAS, EAT FRESH OR DRY

There is yet another well-known class of peas called edible pod
peas. Cultivars such as China Snow Pea, Oregon Sugar Pod or
Amish Snap Pea are eaten fresh off the vine, pod and all. Some
of these are best before the pods start to plump out with peas
(usually referred to as snow peas) and others are great with their
peas formed (usually referred to as snap peas or snack peas).

THE POWER OF PULSES

What is less well known about the edible pod peas is that most make excellent cooking peas when the peas reach a mature size inside the pods and then dry down. Simply shell the peas and cook as you would any other dry pea. I don't really know if they have been used as dry peas in their countries of origin but think they surely must have been because they are so delicious this way. These edible pod peas give you both fresh eating in the summer and hearty soups and stews in the winter.

BUSH AND CLIMBING PEAS

There are many climbing and non-climbing pea cultivars around the world specifically used for drying. Some of these originally came from the monastery gardens of the early Middle Ages.

The peas grown by industrial agriculture are self-supporting bush peas called field peas. These round green or yellow peas are often mechanically divided and sold as split peas. They cook more quickly than whole dry peas.

Shelling peas are among the most popular garden crops and many people choose varieties that need trellising because this makes such an efficient use of space. Growing climbing peas on a trellis about 20 feet (6 m) wide and 7 feet (2 m) tall produces more than a 40-foot (12-m) row of bush peas. Why not grow climbing dry peas as a delicious protein source in your backyard—maybe against a garage or in any small garden space? You will enjoy a big harvest and they will look pretty too.

I believe there is a huge potential for commercial production of climbing peas, with many excellent candidates among both the traditional climbing soup peas and the edible pod peas.

GROWING PEAS ORGANICALLY

Field peas are generally grown with fewer pesticides and herbicides than other crops, but I think it's important to find the varieties that do well without any poisons whatsoever. There are undoubtedly some pea cultivars that are more suited to organic growing methods than others, and those may even include varieties that are now grown with biocides by industrial agriculture. Just because they are grown with toxins now doesn't mean they have to be.

In my organic garden, weevils never penetrate the pod of the Brazilian Snack Pea—it has a thick pod that is nonetheless

Opposite: Trellising climbing peas is a great way to make the most of your garden space. *Carol Pope photo*

Gold Harvest Pea flower.
Photo © Jan Mangan

juicy and crunchy, making it my favourite edible pod pea. It also dries to produce an excellent cooking pea. Other peas that have a similar protection against weevils are Calvert and Japanese Climbing Snow Pea.

We need to grow, share and popularize peas like my hardy Brazilian variety, because the future is going to be not only about food but about unpoisoned food. People around the globe are waking up to the realization that what goes around comes around and if you poison plants and soil you poison humans and all the other creatures on this planet.

PEA TEXTURES AND TASTES

Peas have a wonderful range of textures and tastes. While we're accustomed to sophisticated descriptions of many foods and beverages, including cheeses, meats, beers and wines, peas are overlooked and neglected. Even for coffee, there are connoisseurs who will describe tones of spice, chocolate or fruit, mellowness, crispness and nuttiness. Most of these same descriptions could apply to peas as well: sweetness, smoothness, graininess and robustness should all be part of our vocabulary to describe the delectable and wonderful diversity of peas. If you use Dutch Kapucijner, Century, Kazanskij or other unique soup peas offered by dry pea suppliers, I'm sure you will agree that they each have unique qualities that make them different from commercially available peas.

GOLDS TO BLUES

Few people know of the beautiful colours, shapes and sizes of peas. They don't come in only greens and yellows: in my garden, Swedish Red Peas are a gorgeous hue of claret while my Gold Harvest is a golden treasure. Then there is the Blue Pod Desiree with vibrant purple pods, and the luminous yellow Golden Edible Pod that glows in the garden sunshine. Most of the dry peas I grow have flowers in stunning combinations of pink and purple.

On top of their high nutrition, long and potent track record, beauty and versatility, dry peas also enrich the soil by fixing nitrogen. Productivity improves by simply planting peas in the same place again. How's that for renewable energy!

Last but not least, and this is something that is known and appreciated by new and veteran gardeners alike, peas are easy to grow.

PLANTING PEAS IS A SNAP

I've just planted my first peas of the year as I write this; all I did was plunk them into the ground a couple of inches apart, scruff up the soil so the birds wouldn't notice and write the variety name and date on a stick with a permanent marker. Apart from visiting them as they grow, the next thing to do will be to harvest them in three months!

Peas are a cool-weather crop and it is generally recommended to plant them as soon as the soil can be worked in spring. That's not

Left: Brazilian Snack Pea *(Photo © Jan Mangan).*
Right: Blue Pod Desiree Pea *(Christina Symons photo).*

Peas can be grown in pots for small spaces or balcony gardens. *Carol Pope photos*

such great advice, however, for people who live in coastal climates where the soil can be workable most of the winter. On Canada's West Coast, St. Patrick's Day is the traditional time to plant peas.

Peas can rot in the ground or get set back considerably if the soil is only a few degrees above freezing. Remarkably, though, they can sprout and start growing quickly with temperatures as low as 40F (4C). They'll take about three months to complete their cycle to become dry peas again.

Coastal growers actually have a big window for pea planting because the main concern is avoiding the heat of summer, when most pea afflictions occur. An early-April sowing usually works fine to fully mature peas by mid-July. It's hard to stop pea fanatics, though: I frequently find myself planting peas at the end of February!

For gardeners in most of continental North America, planting as soon as possible is good advice because spring can often become summer in a few weeks. However, home gardeners often have a shady back, front or side yard where peas will stay

cool enough to flourish even in summer. Some growers in hot areas have tremendous success planting peas on cultivated land shaded by trees.

Having said all that, it's important to note that some pea varieties are much more heat tolerant than others. Summer Pea is named accordingly, and Golden Edible Pod is a cultivar from India that can tolerate a lot of warmth.

If you live in a place where temperatures don't go much above 80F (27C), August plantings can work for fall harvests if the weather cooperates. Canada, the US, Europe, China, India, Russia and Australia are all places where summers can be very hot, yet they are the world's leading producers of peas.

Peas thrive in well-drained, rich, sandy and alkaline soil. Because they can rot in cold, wet ground, it is often worthwhile, especially for early plantings, to hill up soil somewhat under pea fencing or in pea beds and loosen it up in general. Adding ashes or dolomite lime when preparing beds often helps too. I have found that peas can do well even in quite acidic ground if it is fertile, and although peas prefer a well-drained soil, they don't mind a moist one.

The twining nature of peas allows them to be planted quite close together; I usually place mine just a couple of inches apart. Natural climbers, there are many low-growing peas that will support themselves simply by grabbing onto their neighbours or that do well with just a few sturdy sticks here and there to cling to. Large commercial acreages are sown with short varieties with no supports, but the home gardener or small farmer can trellis varieties over knee-high for efficiency and abundant yield.

A mechanical row seeder can plant a row as fast as you can walk it. Otherwise, mark rows with an appropriate stick or garden tool and then plunk in the peas 2 inches (5 cm) apart and as deep as they are thick. If, for example, the pea variety is ½ inch (1.25 cm) across, it should be covered with ½ inch (1.25 cm) of soil.

Low-growing peas are often planted in blocks rather than single rows. If the rows are about 1 foot (30 cm) apart, the peas will be able to support each other by clinging together but will still have adequate air circulation. I often use beds that are 4 feet (120 cm) wide and sow three rows of bush peas in them—each plant produces about 300 seeds.

I usually create three rows for my tall-growing peas as well. One row is right below the trellising and the other two are 1 foot (30 cm) away on either side. All can easily reach the support to climb upwards.

I've tended to grow more and more of the climbing peas in the three decades I've been growing them. There are so many interesting varieties and it's convenient to look at them at eye height.

My system uses metal posts and chicken wire; I can put the fencing up in a matter of minutes after I've got the posts in. The chicken wire is usually 2-inch (5-cm) mesh and 6 feet (180 cm) high. I hold it up and weave it as I flip it over and onto the posts, about 10 feet (3 m) apart. You can only weave about a quarter of the height at once because of the tension, so that means you walk back and forth twice. You can use every third or fourth hole for weaving. It's easy to eyeball the holes in the mesh so that you're weaving a vertical line.

Sturdy pea fencing can be used for many years. Because peas fix nitrogen, plants can get a lot more productive in subsequent

Opposite: Purple-podded Pole Peas pulsing! Photo © Jan Mangan

Peas may have delicate flowers but the plants are hardy and vigorous. *Above: Carouby de Maussane Snow Pea* (Photo © Jan Mangan). *Opposite: Mrs. Van's pea* (Christina Symons photo).

years as soil associations build. I often grow peas on the same trellis for three years and then use the same fencing to grow pole beans. There are many other options for facilitating your climbing peas. Wooden or bamboo trellises can be much more attractive than wire on metal posts. There are many kinds of meshes that you can buy or make. I find it advantageous to have the mesh start a few inches above the ground. It makes it easier to sow a middle row and weed there if you need to.

Many books and catalogues recommend annual rotations that have peas in the same garden plot only every fourth year, but I almost always grow peas for three years in the same place! I've yet to experience any pea diseases in all the years I've been growing them, and my crops always do better the second and third year. (I don't know why I don't go for four or five years.) If some kind of pea affliction started to show, I would plant a different crop the next time.

I mulch my peas—mulching keeps weeds to a minimum, makes the soil loose and moist, and reinvigorates the soil when

it's forked under for the next year's planting. I don't normally add other amendments the second and third years unless I feel the soil needs a boost. Then I'll add compost, rock dust or dolomite lime. You have to go easy with composted manure or the pea vines will grow more leaves and fewer peas.

A pleasant thing about peas is that you don't need to thin them. Once they are on their way, grabbing hold of the mesh and linking to each other, you can enjoy their rapid growth, then their pretty flowers and finally the pods that are home to the peas.

DRYING AND SHELLING PEAS

Let the peas dry down completely on the vine. The pods keep their peas dry in the rain and quickly become brittle again when the sun comes out. There will always be a few peas that are not quite finished drying. After picking all the pods, bring them under cover and let them sit on screens for a few more days.

When shelling dry peas (and any other pulse) it is crucial to let the peas dry down completely in the pod rather than opening the pods and putting the peas out to finish drying. They don't dry down well at all if they are exposed to the air and much prefer being in their pod homes to the very end. When peas and other beans are sufficiently dry, they are so hard that you can't make an indentation with a fingernail.

Shelling peas by hand can be an enjoyable activity to share with friends. It's also fun to do with your feet. I use my threshing box (see Drying Pods, Threshing Pulses, page 38, for more on this). Walking on the brittle pods and rubbing them against the slats releases the seeds in just a few minutes. Then it's a matter of screening the chaff or blowing it away. The right meshes can let the small chaff through first and then the peas without the larger chaff.

I use the blow nozzle attachment on my air compressor, cleaning the peas in seconds. A small fan or blow-dryer also works well. There is little danger of blowing the peas away because they are so much heavier than the pod debris.

Next, it's time to put the threshed peas back on their screens and do some quality control, namely to pick out any peas that have holes in them, are misshapen or have weevils. (It's okay to compost all of these.) Some pea varieties are more subject

Opposite: Harry Burton's Shelling Pea was happy to grow in the same place as the year before. *Chris Thoreau photo*

The pods and peas of Calvert peas are sweet, juicy and crunchy. If you can resist snacking on them all and let some dry on the vine, they make delicious soup peas. *Left: Photo by Chris Thoreau. Right: Photo © Jan Mangan.*

to weevils than others, but you'll almost always harvest some with obvious weevil damage or a few weevils or both. Once left with only your good peas, it's best to leave them in the air for a few more days to ensure every last one is dry and won't become mouldy in storage.

This is perhaps the most special moment of all in growing your own dry pea crop: the freshly harvested and shelled peas are gorgeous and bestow their glow on you.

Then there's the eating!

SOAKING AND SIMMERING PEAS

As with all pulses, the procedure is simple. Put them in a pot or bowl and cover them with a few times their volume of water. Stir to encourage any debris or imperfect peas to rise to the surface. Pour off the floaters. Soak the peas overnight and rinse them again before putting them in a pot with three or more times their volume of water. Heat to boiling and then simmer until the peas are cooked to the desired consistency.

The cooking time will vary considerably depending on size, variety, freshness and soaking time. It may fluctuate from 40 to 80 minutes but is usually about an hour. As with all the pulses, peas toughen with age and then take longer to absorb water and cook. It's best to cook all dry peas and beans within a year of harvest.

The optimum cooking time involves familiarity with your peas and the way you want to eat them. Especially if you're cooking your peas to eat whole (rather than blended), there is a point where the skin merges perfectly with the flesh to provide just the right combination of textures.

I often taste test my cooked peas by trying them unadorned right out of the pot, then seeing what they are like with some butter or oil and a bit of seasoning. Then I'm ready to imagine how best they might be used in recipes. With just oil and seasoning, however, they are great as a side dish for practically any meal.

Purple-podded Pole Pea.
Carol Pope photo

CHAPTER 5

Favas

With favas *(Vicia faba)*, I want to begin where I left off with peas, namely the cooking of them. I believe the main reason favas are undervalued in North America has to do with their preparation. As with dry peas, there is an optimum cooking time with favas that leaves them with the best texture and this is generally about 90 minutes.

There aren't many fava aficionados in North America. Almost every reference to cooking favas says to peel their skins or you'll be sorry. This is a shame. While the outer skin is certainly much more of an issue with favas than peas—if you slightly undercook fava beans, or overcook them, this will cause the skin to be tough and unpleasant to chew—as with most other cooked foods, the best results come when you pay attention to timing.

FAVAS IN ANCIENT EGYPT

Favas have been around and appreciated for as long as peas. They were grown by the ancient Egyptians and Chinese, as well as the Greeks and Romans. A mainstay of the European diet until the 16th century, they are now eaten daily by millions of people in the Middle East, India, Burma, Mexico and Brazil.

You can cook up fresh favas like fresh peas, before they get woody or tough. Simply sauté or steam them for 5 to 8 minutes and then season with salt, pepper and a touch of butter and any herbs you particularly like.

Opposite, clockwise from top left: Sweet Lorane Fava, Purple Flowered Fava, Andy's Broad Bean, Purple Fava Bean, Jim Ternier's Fava, Sunshine Fava.

Left: Most fava flowers are black and white (*Photo courtesy patjo/Shutterstock.com*).
Right: Tic beans, or bell bean favas, have short pods and small seeds compared to their larger fava/broad bean cousins (*Photo © Jan Mangan*).

It is fascinating to read about the many traditional and diverse fava preparations around the globe, like *baghali ghatogh*, *douban-jiang* and *fasolada soupa*.

COLD HARDY, HALE AND HEARTY

Favas are the hardiest of the pulses. They are a tenacious and trouble-free crop that succeeds where the growing season is short and other beans would fail. They survive temperatures as low as 6F (-14C), require very little water as long as they get off to a decent start in early spring, and are easy to grow and very productive.

Like peas, they can even be planted again in late summer in areas where winters are cool but not much below freezing. In the spring, plant them February through March; in late summer, plant September through October.

BIG BEANS, PURPLE TO BUFF

I'm often asked if fava beans are the same as broad beans. People who grow "broad beans" are usually referring to a large-seeded fava that is shelled as a fresh bean. They are especially known as such in Australia and England. Two of the most famous varieties are Exhibition Long Pod and Broad Windsor. As with shelling peas, these "broad beans" aren't always good when dried. However, there are many large fava cultivars that are.

The large kidney-shaped favas are the biggest beans around, and they come in many colours, including brown, buff, olive,

green and purple. Many cultures or regions cultivate one variety and aren't familiar with others.

It's difficult in North America to source diverse types but I've started to offer a selection of some especially delicious varieties. One is called "Andy's Broad Bean," named after Andy Pollock, who lives near a small town called Houston in northern British Columbia. He's made selections of it for over 30 years and now I do too. The seed is a radiant shade of green and produces abundant amounts of rich-tasting dry beans for cooking.

Another fava that has been popular in the Salt Spring Seeds catalogue for many years is a bright purple one I call "Purple Fava." Until a few years ago, I thought that, like this favourite, all purple-seeded favas originated from Central America. Then my friend George Laundry gave me some. He had kept these going from the time he was a kid in Wales, and says they have been very common fare there for hundreds of years, so I've named this one "Welsh Fava." The plants are a bit smaller and have beautiful purple flowers.

There is also a Crimson-flowered Fava from England that is green-seeded and makes an excellent cooking bean. Most fava flowers, however, are white with distinctive black centres.

I think that some of the best favas are the small-seeded cultivars normally grown in North America as cover crops. These are referred to as tic beans, bell beans or field beans. Their seeds are more like large peas than the huge kidney shape of other favas

Left: Fava seeds come in a wide variety of hues (*Christina Symons photo*). *Right:* The seeds of Jim Ternier's Fava have some chocolate coloration and also have a rich chocolate flavour as a cooked dried bean (*photo © Jan Mangan*).

and, from what I've seen, come in even more diverse colours. One that I've named after Jim Ternier, who gifted it to me, has rich olive and brown tones and a chocolate-like flavour.

You are probably getting the idea by now that a lot of the names given to pulses are somewhat arbitrary. Unlike the names for heirloom varieties of many other crops that have been kept sacrosanct by seed savers for generations, pulses have been so overlooked that most lack traceable identification. I recently obtained a wonderful large-seeded heritage fava from the Sunshine Coast of BC, for which no one had a name. So I'm calling it "Sunshine Fava." I called a broad bean "Mrs. Barton's" for many years until I was told that it was *Mr.* Barton's prized cultivar.

Most cultivated favas grow 4 to 5 feet (120 to 150 cm) high, with succulent-looking blue-green leaves on thick, pulpy stalks. The flowers have a strong and sweet scent that is attractive to bees and other pollinators. The pods that splay out from the stem vary considerably in length in cultivars, some being up to a foot (30 cm) long.

SOWING FAVAS, SPRING AND SUMMER

In coastal and southern areas of North America, favas can be planted in spring or late summer. They are even hardier than peas. For spring sowings they can be planted as soon as the ground can be worked in the spring. Light frost will not harm young plants. For overwintering favas, mid-August to mid-September sowings work well.

Because fava blossoms will fall off before setting pods if temperatures go much above 70F (21C), they won't mature seeds in places where hot summers come on quickly. Strategies that prolong pea harvests also work for favas, such as planting in shadier areas, hilling soil around the base of plants, mulching and keeping the soil moist.

Favas grow successfully in many different soils, even heavy clay. Unlike other legumes, they can thrive in soils with high salinity. They shouldn't need fertilizer if grown in built-up garden soil. They do best in well-cultivated ground that is high in phosphorous and potassium and, like peas, prefer soil that is not too acidic.

Opposite: At this stage, these Purple Fava beans would be good shelled and steamed. *Photo © Jan Mangan*

When sowing favas it's often helpful to soak the seeds overnight. Though not essential, this ensures quick and even germination. In garden beds, the seeds should be sown 1 to 2 inches (2.5 to 5 cm) deep and about 6 inches (15 cm) apart. I'll often thin plants to about 1 foot (30 cm) apart because they do get very large. The rows should definitely be a foot (30 cm) or more apart.

Fava beans compete poorly with weeds until they start to tower above them. In the early stages, they can benefit considerably from mulching or from soil drawn around the base of the plants with a rake or hoe. None of the varieties I've grown so far have required support, but in windy places it might be worthwhile staking each end of the row and enclosing the beans with string.

Watering is seldom necessary with favas unless spring is unusually dry. They are resistant to both diseases and pests. Their most common problem is aphids. It is often recommended to control aphids by using insecticidal soap or by pinching off plant tops. I find that aphids will usually congregate on a small percentage of plants and then leave the rest alone. I mostly ignore aphids, though there has been the occasional time I've sprayed them off with a hose. This is usually not necessary, though, as wasps, ladybugs and other helpful insects often arrive quickly on the scene to deal admirably with aphids.

HARVESTING FAVAS, EAT NOW OR LATER

When the pods are well formed and deep green, favas can be shelled and steamed fresh. To harvest the dry beans, you need to wait until the pods darken and become brittle. Unlike other pulses, fava plants can take more than three weeks for all the pods to become ready to pick. The pods at the base of the plants blacken first.

Farmers usually cut field favas before they all ripen. The home gardener can wait to pick until half the pods have dried black, usually by the end of July. The weather of late July and early August most often enables a few leisurely harvests. However, if left standing too long in hot weather, the pods of some varieties will shatter with the beans falling to the ground.

A fingernail won't dent the beans when they are sufficiently dry. They can be shelled by hand or threshed by foot in a box or on a tarp.

You can expect favas to normally yield over 10 pounds (4.5 kg) per 50 feet (15 m).

SOAKING AND SIMMERING

A few people, usually males of Mediterranean descent, experience a hereditary allergic reaction when they eat fresh (rather than dried) fava beans or inhale fava pollen.

The most notable symptom of "favism" is jaundice in response to destruction of red blood cells, which usually disappears without treatment within a few days. Where fava beans are a dietary staple, allergies to them are detected as a matter of course. The possibility of allergic reaction if you haven't had them before is worth bearing in mind.

Cooks usually recommend a long soaking and many hours of cooking for favas. This is because most commercially available beans have aged and dried considerably before reaching the consumer. I have found that all the favas I've grown require about 90 minutes of simmering after an overnight soak. Cooking can be shortened a little with a 24-hour soak.

Favas produce a lot of pods and a lot of beans. Ten plants could easily give you over 4 pounds (1.8 kg) of dried beans.
Photo © Jan Mangan

As stated at the beginning of this chapter, it is important not to overcook favas or the seed coat will separate and become very tough. Most varieties have a seed coat that retains a chewiness that is quite pleasant if optimally cooked.

Because they have such an earthy and meaty flavour, just a few dozen cooked favas can add richness, depth and delightful flavour to many soups. And, as with dry peas, dry favas can be savoured very satisfactorily with a little seasoning and some oil or butter. A simple dish called *ful medames* is eaten by millions of people in Mediterranean and Middle Eastern countries as their morning breakfast; in fact, it is considered to be one of Egypt's national dishes.

SAVING SEEDS, PLANNING PLANTINGS

Favas are mostly self-fertile but can be cross-pollinated by insects more than the other pulses. To maintain pure strains, plant only one variety or stagger plantings so that different cultivars are not flowering at the same time.

Fava seeds, like those of the other pulses, will easily last for four to five years as long as they are kept dry, cool and out of the light. Given that favas have been and continue to be popular in cultures around the world, it seems they could and should easily catch on in North America as well. In areas where summers are warm but not too hot, or where winters are cool but not much below freezing, they are an incredibly hardy, prolific and rewarding crop.

Ful Medames

Cook **1 cup (250 mL) soaked dry fava beans** until soft, about 50 minutes if homegrown, longer if store-bought. Drain well. Dress with ¼ cup (60 mL) olive oil (or flax oil), **juice of ½ lemon** and **2 cloves crushed garlic**. If desired, add dill, chopped onion, cayenne pepper or chopped parsley to season. Let cool and serve with hard-boiled eggs.

CHAPTER 6
Lentils

For millennia, lentils *(Lens culinaris)* have traditionally been eaten with barley and wheat—these three foodstuffs originated in the same regions and spread through Africa and Europe as people migrated. Before the first century, they were introduced into India, a country that still has high regard for the spiced lentil dish known as *dahl*. Lentils are enormously important in many other parts of the world, especially Africa, Asia and the Mediterranean.

The leading global producers of lentils are Canada, India, Australia and Turkey. Canada harvests about a third of world production annually, almost all of it in the province of Saskatchewan, with most of it exported. The most important lentil-producing areas in the US are the Palouse region of eastern Washington and the Idaho panhandle.

BABYLONIAN BREAD

One of the first foods to have ever been cultivated, lentils are believed to have originated in central Asia and have been consumed since prehistoric times. Ten-thousand-year-old lentil remains have been uncovered on the banks of the Euphrates River in what is now northern Syria. The remnants of a paste of lentils were found in 3rd-century BC tombs at Thebes, and a 2nd-century BC fresco shows lentil soup being prepared in the time of Ramses II. Lentils were also mentioned in the Bible: Jacob

Opposite, clockwise from top left: Large Green Lentil, Le Puy Green Lentil, Black Beluga Lentil, Crimson Lentil, Red Lentil.

Lentils have small pods that usually contain two seeds. *Carol Pope photo*

traded them to Esau for his birthright, and they were eaten as bread by the Jewish people during their captivity in Babylon.

SOWING LENTILS

Lentils produce small and very branching plants, forming tufts 2 feet (60 cm) or more. Unlike peas and favas, their small white or pale blue flowers are hardly noticeable. The flowers are produced in pairs and succeeded by flat pods, each of which usually contains two seeds. Colours range from yellow to red-orange to green, brown and black. They are sold in many forms, with or without the skins, whole or split.

Lentils are closely related to peas and, like them, do best in cool, moist, sandy loam. Like all pulse crops, they are hardy and easy-to-grow nitrogen fixers that can be planted soon after the soil is workable in the spring. Like other pulses, they are super-high in protein, vitamins and minerals.

I now list seven lentil varieties in my Salt Spring Seeds catalogue. Given that lentils are such a reliable and nutritious

crop, it's amazing to me that no other gardening catalogue offers them.

I have large and small, red and green cultivars, a crimson lentil, and two black varieties called "Le Puy" and "Black Beluga." Their size varies from ⅛ to ¼ inch (0.13 to 0.6 cm) across, so they are much tinier than the other pulses. Unlike peas, which can stand being planted as close as 1 inch (2.5 cm) apart, the final spacing for lentils should be 4 to 5 inches (10 to 13 cm). It's hard for this gardener to plant such small seeds that far apart, so I usually have to thin my lentils considerably. They seem best planted just below the surface in freshly worked soil. Lentils don't compete well with weeds at the beginning, so mulch them early after weeding. An excellent way to plant lentils is to start them in 4-inch (10-cm) pots that are protected from the birds (see Hungry Birds and Pests, page 34) and then transplant them to their final spacing once they are about 3 inches (7.5 cm) high. Their initial root system is small enough to do this without interrupting growth, and this saves seeds and lessens thinning and initial weeding.

Lentils can be started early in pots and transplanted when they get to be about this high. *Carol Pope photo*

QUICK HARVEST, BEST THRESH

My lentil harvests are usually in mid-summer, a time when there is little concern about the seeds getting wet, but there is the possibility that some of the pods could shatter in the heat. You don't want to be picking lentils off the ground! It was only last season that I learned to cut the plants at ground level when most of the seeds were ready, and to let them finish a bit more on a tarp in my greenhouse. Pulling lentil pods off the plants by hand is a far more tedious exercise than picking the other, larger pulses.

Lentils are easily and quickly threshed by walking on the entire plants after all the seeds are well dried down. To do this, I process them in my threshing box (see Drying Pods, Threshing Pulses, page 38). I then remove all the large debris from the box and blow away the remaining chaff with the air nozzle on my compressor. The same cleaning process can be completed almost as easily using appropriate screens.

As I always do with my pulses, I lay out the cleaned seeds on mesh screens in a greenhouse where I inspect the lentils and discard any dubious ones. I give all the remaining lentils a few days on the screens so that every last one is totally dried. Then I store them in sealed bottles in a cool, dry, dark place for future use.

SOUPS AND STEWS, SALADS OR SIDES

In the Middle East, lentils are most often used in soups and stews and they are frequently flavoured with lemon, olive oil and garlic. In south India, where they are a major source of protein, many methods are used to prepare lentils for breads, fritters, salads and vegetable dishes.

Lentils have a distinctive earthy flavour. They are frequently combined with rice, which has a similar cooking time. A lentil and rice dish, usually garnished with fried onions, is referred to in the Middle East as *mujaddara* or *mejadra*. Rice and lentils are also cooked together in *khichdi*, a popular dish in Pakistan and India. A similar dish, *kushari*—a tasty mixture of lentils, rice, pasta, tomato sauce, chickpeas and garlic—is considered one of two national dishes in Egypt and is standard lunchtime fare there. Lentils are used to prepare inexpensive and nutritious soups all over Europe and South America.

Unlike other pulses, lentils need no soaking and cook relatively quickly. When boiling lentils, add 3 cups (710 mL) water for each cup (250 mL) of lentils. Add the lentils to boiling water, and when the water returns to a boil, turn down the heat to simmer and cover. Add a bay leaf for flavour. The varieties I grow take from 20 to 40 minutes to cook. They must be watched because they soften easily and can lose their texture.

Cooking times can be adjusted depending on the intended use. If you are going to be serving lentils in a salad or soup and desire a firmer texture, remove them 5 to 10 minutes earlier than their usual cooking time. If you are preparing something that requires a mushier consistency, such as a dahl, the lentils will likely benefit from an additional 10 to 15 minutes. To eat lentils in the most basic way, remove the bay leaf and add a little butter, lemon juice and seasoning such as pepper or paprika. For my favourite lentil soup combinations, see Dan's Salt Spring Garden Soups (page 144).

Canada is the world's largest exporter of lentils, most of which are grown in Saskatchewan. It's time Canadians grew more lentils for themselves.
Left: Photo courtesy Karen Kaspar/Shutterstock.com.
Right: Photo courtesy Lorraine Swanson/Shutterstock.com

CHAPTER 7

Chickpeas

Chickpeas (*Cicer arietinum*) are also known as garbanzos or garbanzo beans. Quite an unknown fact in North America is that chickpeas are as delicious as shelling peas when eaten fresh. In Ethiopia, I often saw children selling branches of chickpeas by the roadsides before the plants had started to dry down; they are considered a special treat to pop right into the mouth.

As with lentils, Canada exports a huge amount of chickpeas all over the world. Most production is in Saskatchewan and southeastern Alberta. Sadly (I think), Canada also *imports* a lot of chickpeas. You can't find Canadian-grown garbanzos in most grocery or health food stores in Canada, but you can find chickpeas from Mexico, India and other far-off farms. And, although they are grown on more than two hundred thousand acres in the US, primarily in California, Idaho, Montana and Washington, few Americans eat their own chickpeas.

FALCON FACES

Chickpeas have been grown in Mediterranean countries for ten thousand years. They were known by the name "falcon face" in ancient Egypt. The Romans used the word *arietinum* (ram-like) to describe this roundish, compressed seed that somewhat resembles a ram's head with horns curling over the sides. *Cicer arietinum* was a staple of their diet and still plays a

Opposite, clockwise from top left: Desi Chickpea, Black Kabuli Chickpea, Chestnut Chickpea, Winnifred's Garbanzo, Edible Island Chickpea, Chickpea of Spello.

In North America, shelled fresh chickpeas are a yet-to-be-discovered treat. *Photos © Jan Mangan*

very important part in the regional cooking of southern Europe. Chickpeas are widely grown in India and Burma, where they rival wheat in acreage under cultivation.

GROWING CHICKPEAS, PLACING PLANTS

The chickpea is a graceful and delicate-looking plant that branches near the ground and is usually about 2 feet (60 cm) high. About 4 months from the time of sowing, 1 to 2 seeds are borne in each of the numerous round swollen pods. It is quite a substantial plant that spreads more than 1 foot (30 cm) in all directions.

Like peas, favas and lentils, chickpeas are a cool-weather crop. Seeds can be sown once the temperature stays over 40F (4C), which in most places means they are best planted in late March to mid-April. They can tolerate frost in the cold season and even withstand high summer temperatures during flowering.

The plants are best grown in rows 18 inches (46 cm) apart and thinned to about 1 foot (30 cm) apart because of their spreading habit. They require little attention beyond the occasional weeding or hoeing and are quite drought-tolerant. I normally mulch my rows of chickpeas once they are 2 to 3 inches (5 to 7.5 cm) high; then I don't have to do anything for them until harvest. They don't need staking, and in fact are so robust that I'll often plant a row of bush peas just a foot (30 cm) away so that the tendrils of the peas can cling to the chickpeas to stay upright.

THE SHELLING SHUFFLE

The dry pods of chickpeas are more difficult to process than those of other beans because the shells have a lanolin-like stickiness and cave in rather than split apart when hand-threshed. So placing them on a tarp or in a large box or rubber bin and doing "the shuffle" on them is the way to go. For more information, see Drying Pods, Threshing Pulses on page 38.

As with other pulses, they should be stored in a cool, dry and dark place.

CHESTNUT CHICKPEAS, WINNIFRED'S GARBANZO

I've been experimenting with chickpeas for quite a number of years. One of the varieties I've maintained is the large-seeded Chestnut, the only cream-coloured cultivar commonly available in North America. I also have a similarly sized black garbanzo that hails from Afghanistan and is called "Kabuli." My friend Rupert Adams brought back a standard Indian chickpea gifted to him by Vandana Shiva at her Navdanya Institute in India. This chickpea, called "Desi," is a smaller, dark-brown seed and has become one of my favourites due to its flavour, production and reliability.

Another favourite for similar reasons is Winnifred's Garbanzo. Winnifred had already been growing it for 30 years before she shared some seeds with me 20 years ago. Although I did not have the chance to meet her in person before she died, we spoke on the

Most people, seeing chickpeas growing for the first time, remark on their grace and beauty. *Karen Mouat photo*

Left: At harvest time, garbanzos rattle in their pods (*Karen Mouat photo*). *Right:* The flowers of Black Kabuli Chickpeas are a pretty pink and white (*Photo © Jan Mangan*). *Opposite:* Chickpea pods have a lanolin-like coating that keeps dew and rain out. *Karen Mouat photo*

phone dozens of times and I was always inspired by how self-sufficient she was, living totally off the grid in a very remote area of BC.

As with dry peas, favas and lentils, you'll be hard-pressed to find chickpeas offered in any garden seed catalogues. I've been doing my best to change that!

CHICKPEA CHAPATI, CONDIMENTS AND CURRY

Around the world, chickpeas are used in a wide variety of snacks, soups, sweets, curries and condiments, and are well known for their tastiness in such foods as dhal and tabbouleh. They are also ground to produce a fine flour called *besan* to make roti or chapati; this flour is wonderful for those who are gluten intolerant, and useful for making virtually all types of breads, for baking and even for pancakes. In the Middle East, chickpeas have long been widely consumed as hummus. See Miso and Charred Scallion Hummus (page 126) for a new twist on traditional hummus recipes.

If you're used to preparing dishes with dry or canned chickpeas, you'll be surprised and delighted at the difference when you use homegrown ones. As with other garden-fresh beans, their taste is mild and sweet and cooking times are considerably less than is usually recommended. For fresh chickpeas, 1½ hours of simmering (rather than the standard 2½ hours) after an overnight soak will be sufficient.

CHAPTER 8

Beans

By "beans," I am referring to what the Food and Agricultural Organization of the United Nations calls the common bean or *Phaseolus vulgaris*. These include pinto, kidney, navy and chili beans, plus a host of other soup, baking, salad and refry beans.

BEAN TRAVELLING

Unlike the other pulses described so far, these beans are warm-weather crops and their origins are in Central and South America. Columbus found these beans growing in America, and their cultivation had been going on for thousands of years before then. He brought them to Europe and, during the 16th and 17th centuries, they became more popular than other beans such as favas, and then early settlers brought them to North America.

GARDEN GOODNESS

Almost all dry beans available in supermarkets today are imported and old stock. We have not learned to value subtle differences in beans the way some of us do for coffees or teas, cheeses or meats, beers or wines. North Americans often regard cultures that eat a lot of beans as being sadly deprived of the meat and dairy products we love so much. It's time we became much more impressed by the flavours and versatility of pulses,

Opposite, from left to right. Top row: Teggia Bush Dry Bean, Beka Brown, Black Turtle, Borlotti Bean; *second row:* Ireland Creek Annie, Hutterite Soup Bean, Calypso, Pinks Bush Dry Bean; *third row:* Candy, Aztec Red Kidney, Tiger Eye, Orca; *bottom row:* Ruckle, Black Coco.

in addition to their nutrition, easy care and storage, and benefits to the earth.

There are dozens of high-yielding, short-season and great-tasting bean varieties not offered by stores. As with almost all homegrown food, your own dry beans will taste better than store-bought varieties. Not only are garden-grown beans more easily digested, they also cajole you to highlight their taste rather than burying it under condiments and spices.

GROWING DRY BEANS, USING TRELLISES AND TEEPEES

As with peas, there are bush and pole varieties of dry beans. Although pole varieties are too labour intensive for commercial agriculture, they offer the home gardener great opportunity to grow a lot of high-quality protein in a small amount of space. Pole beans grow 6 to 10 feet (1.8 to 3 m) tall by twining around sticks, strings or wires, and look striking in the garden. Strong supports such as trellises, fences and teepees are best set in place before the seeds are sown.

Opposite: Ricci's Pole Bean. Pole beans can provide a lot of high quality food in a small amount of space (*Karen Mouat photo*). *Above:* Auntie Vie's Italian Pole Bean growing on a trellis. *Chris Thoreau photos*

It's quite exciting to see the first bean leaves erupt. *Carol Pope photo*

Some nitrogen is important for good bean growth but as with peas, favas, lentils and chickpeas, beans can fix their own nitrogen from the air through the action of the *Rhizobium* bacteria that live in nodules on their roots. Thus beans are an excellent crop for enriching your soil. In a new garden, it's worth coating your bean seed with an inoculant containing the proper type of *Rhizobium* if you can find it at a local garden shop or through a seed catalogue (see Nitrogen Nodules, Bacteria Boosters, page 29).

When choosing a planting site for dry beans, it's worth remembering that they take about six weeks longer to reach full maturity than fresh green beans. Because you want to harvest the pods at maximum dryness, plant them where they will continue to receive sun during September afternoons.

Because beans are a warm-weather crop, there is little to be gained by having them shiver through their early growth. On the coast of British Columbia where I garden, I wait to plant them until at least early May to ensure quick, even germination. For much of North America, the last week in May is the optimum sowing time.

On a small scale, planting beans in raised beds saves a lot of space and enables the soil to warm more quickly in spring. I plant my dry beans in rows about 18 inches (46 cm) apart. This allows me to do most of my weeding by hoeing between the rows until the beans grow large enough to suppress the weeds. I sow the seed about 1 inch (2.5 cm) deep, using my push row seeder. (This is an efficient and inexpensive tool for large gardens that I also use to sow bush peas and chickpeas.)

You might have noticed that I've hardly touched on diseases and pests that you might encounter in growing the various pulses. That's because, except for a few aphids (simply spray them off) and bean beetles (hand-picking works best), I haven't seen any in the 30 years I've been growing them.

By planting in earth that has been freshly tilled or dug, I often don't have to hoe again for weed control. I'm a strong advocate of mulch and usually spread straw or hay around my beans and over the entire growing area as soon the beans are 3 to 4 inches (7.5 to 10 cm) high. This not only allows the beans to grow without weed competition, it keeps the soil loose and moist and adds a lot of organic matter to the soil when it's worked in later on.

I plant my bush and pole beans about 1 inch (2.5 cm) deep and about 6 inches (15 cm) apart. For pole beans, I plant one row under the trellis and two outer rows 1 foot (30 cm) from this centre row.

The cool-weather pulses discussed in this book mature in the heat of summer, which usually allows them to dry to perfection in

Bean pods give cheery garden greetings for many weeks. *Left:* Honey Wax Bean (*Carol Pope photo*). *Right:* Tongue of Fire Bean (*Karen Mouat photo*).

the garden. With warm-weather beans, it's best to grow early-maturing varieties so they can dry down in their pods by late August or early September. That is, unless you live where cool weather and rain don't start until later on.

HARVESTING AND THRESHING

As with other beans, you have to watch that warm-weather beans don't start spilling out of their pods on especially hot days. Many varieties don't ripen all at once and I'll often do several pickings of the most mature beans. I bring them indoors to a warm, dry place with good air circulation, let them dry a few days longer, then thresh them by hand or foot.

Some longer-season varieties do not reach the drying stage until mid-September or early October. If rain or fog moves in, pull entire plants and bring them into a well-ventilated green-house, shed, barn, attic or basement. Most books say to hang them upside down but I think they can be stood upright or just spread out on a flat surface as long as there is good air circulation. It's amazing the way the plants will suck energy up the stem to complete the maturation process.

It's important to *not* open the pods to make the beans dry faster. Let them dry down completely in their pods to the point that they are like little stones and a fingernail can't make a dent in them.

For years, I threshed my beans by hand, usually with friends helping. You get to be quite fast and can carry on exciting conversations at the same time. Now I use my threshing box and do my shuffle on them and sometimes other people get in the box with me. It takes only a few minutes in the box to thresh a significant amount of beans (see page 38 for more details).

CREAMY AND CRUNCHY, SWEET AND NUTTY

Early on in my bean-tasting times, I developed a simple system for comparing the flavours and textures of different cultivars. It is one I still use: eating them plain, with no seasoning.

After an overnight soaking, I pour fresh water over them, bring the water to the boil, then simmer them with the lid slightly open. Most homegrown beans need only 50 minutes to cook, so I scoop

Opposite: Many pole beans have a lot of seeds in a pod. *Photo © Jan Mangan*

up a couple with a spoon after 45 minutes to see what they are like. Then I try them again every 5 minutes.

Beans vary so much in texture and flavour. For example, the common white navy bean has practically no taste and a texture that leaves everything to be desired. In comparison, a larger white bean called "Ruckle," which has been in my Salt Spring Seeds catalogue from the beginning, has a wonderful creamy and crunchy texture plus a sweet, nutty taste. I use it as a base for one of my favourite salad dressings; see page 133 for the recipe.

Most beans that are used fresh don't make good dry beans at all. Unless you jazzed them up with a lot of your favourite seasoning, you wouldn't enjoy heritage green beans such as Venture, Tendergreen, Provider or Blue Lake as cooked dry beans. Salt Spring Seeds has some beans that are awesome both fresh and dry. Blooming Prairie, Tanya's Pink Pod and Blue Jay all make wonderful snacks right in the garden and taste good both cooked fresh and dry.

Taking the time to taste-test your dry beans without any adornment gives you the opportunity to imagine what they would be like in salads, soups, sauces and sides. Depending on the type of dish you are preparing, you can learn to finely adjust cooking times to result in the texture you want.

Great-tasting bean soups can be made with little more than cooked beans, garlic or onions, and vegetables. Large, mild-flavoured beans, such as Soldier, Money, Maine Yellow Eye,

Opposite: Blooming Prairie bean has glowing pods as well as pretty flowers. Its mauve and white dry bean is also sweet eye candy (*Photo © Jan Mangan*). *Above:* The flowers of Blooming Prairie bean are as vibrant as the pods that develop from them (*Chris Thoreau photo*).

Molasses Face and Ruckle, will readily absorb whatever seasonings and spices are added. More flavourful beans, such as Nez Perce, Ireland Creek Annie or Hutterite, yield their own tasty broths. For some of my favourite bean soup combinations, see Dan's Salt Spring Garden Soups on page 144.

Certain beans almost ask you to prepare them in certain ways. Black Turtle beans are great for curries and Red Kidney beans make delicious chili.

An important tip in cooking beans is to not attempt to soften and flavour them at the same time by cooking them in a sauce—particularly one with salt or acidic ingredients such as tomatoes. This slows the tenderizing process down considerably. When you add precooked beans to a sauce, their texture will not deteriorate and they will happily absorb the new flavours.

You can, however, add garlic, onion or herbs to the cooking water right from the start—this will not impede your pulses from becoming tender and will add flavour.

There are so many beans and so many recipes for them (and you'll find some especially delectable ones in this book!), that by growing or sourcing some of these beauties you will have a world of flavour at your fingertips.

SEED-SAVING ADVENTURES

Common beans are self-fertile so it's rare to see any crosses. If you do find a mutant bean plant, it can be very fun and interesting to see what the seeds from it will produce the next time around. I've gone on some fascinating bean journeys the few times that this has happened to me, one of which was with Tanya's Pink Pod. Tanya, a garden apprentice in 1998, spotted two bushes of beans with phosphorescent pink pods in a row of Sequoia beans with their normal green pods. We saved the seeds, and the following year, all the plants produced the same strikingly gorgeous pods. The pods are exceptionally good both fresh and steamed (and turn the usual green when cooked), and the seeds are nutty and creamy as a cooked dry bean. They've been in my Salt Spring Seeds catalogue ever since.

Opposite: Eaten fresh off the bush, Tanya's Pink Pod is crisp, juicy and full of bean flavour. *Photo* © *Jan Mangan*

Recipes

STORING AND COOKING PULSES

Dry peas and beans, chickpeas, favas and lentils don't have to be refrigerated, frozen, canned or packaged in plastic. They store well in closed bottles and plastic containers, and the most important consideration in storing pulses is simply to keep them dry. Avoid storing them in paper bags, which absorb moisture. They should be kept cool and in a dark place if possible.

Your homegrown pulses will cook quicker and be more digestible than store-bought ones. As pulses age and oxidize, they shrivel, lose colour and don't absorb water as readily as when they are soaked before cooking. It is best to use pulses within a year. (Just in time for your next season's harvest!)

Although pulses don't make for optimum eating after about a year, they usually stay viable as seed for four to five years.

Prior to soaking or cooking your pulses, remove any small pebbles or other foreign debris, along with shrivelled or broken seeds.

Lentils are the only pulses that do not require soaking; simply rinse them prior to cooking.

As part of the soaking process, I suggest you rinse your pulses two to three times to avoid the flatulence factor (see page 25).

PULSE SOAKING AND COOKING TIMES

While cooking times will vary considerably depending on the size, variety, freshness and soaking time of your pulses, this list provides a general guide for cooking pulses within a year of their harvest. Older pulses, and particularly chickpeas, are harder and take longer to absorb water and cook, sometimes needing another half hour to even an extra full hour. Adequately cooked pulses should be soft, not tough and chewy, and tender enough to dissolve easily in your mouth.

For all soaking, add a minimum of 3 cups (710 mL) water for each cup (250 mL) of pulses. For an overnight soak, use cold water and keep the pulses in the refrigerator. After soaking, rinse the pulses and bring a minimum of three times their volume of water to a boil. Add pulses, return to the boil, then simmer as follows:

- Peas: soak overnight, simmer 1 hour
- Beans: soak overnight, simmer 50 minutes
- Chickpeas: soak overnight, simmer 1½ hours
- Favas: soak overnight, simmer 1½ hours
- Lentils: simmer 20–40 minutes

Each cup (250 mL) of dry pulses yields 2 to 3 cups (475 to 710 mL) when cooked.
  Store cooked pulses in the refrigerator for up to 5 days or keep them ready in 1-cup (250-mL) portions in the freezer for your favourite recipes. You can also purée cooked pulses prior to freezing. It makes sense to have some ready to go for dips like hummus (page 126) or other quick-to-make pulse recipes.

While simmering, check the pot periodically to ensure that it does not boil dry, or add extra water as a precaution. If you have liquid to spare once your pulses are cooked, save it for your next batch of soup by storing it in the freezer.

If you are in a hurry, you can give pulses a quick soak. Bring them to the boil in a saucepan and boil gently for 2 minutes; then remove from the heat, cover and leave them to sit for 1 hour before cooking them.

Warning: While it's fine to use a slow cooker to simmer your presoaked pulses, they must be boiled on the stovetop for 10 to 12 minutes first. Pulses, particularly beans, contain a toxic compound called phytohemagglutinin (PHA), which dissipates with cooking (this is not an issue for fresh green beans, however). A slow cooker on its own does not heat the pulses adequately to ensure they are optimal for eating.

FLAVOUR FULL, TEXTURE RICH

All the pulses make a really good meal with nothing added except salt, pepper and a good dash of oil. You will also find that there is a world of flavour available to you when you cook with pulses:

- Peas have their unique pea essence that goes so well with carrots and onions.
- Beans offer a wide range of tastes and textures. The lighter-coloured varieties are usually mild and absorb the flavours of other ingredients while the black and red beans have their own spiciness that marries happily with cumin or chili.
- Fava beans have an assertive meaty flavour and require very little adornment to supplement their richness.
- Chickpeas and lentils merge wonderfully with a host of seasonings, spices and cooked vegetables.

SPROUTING PULSES, BOOSTING HEALTH

By sprouting your own homegrown pulses, or organic pulses from a local source, you can enjoy an ongoing supply of crunchy, healthy sprouts for salads, wraps, sandwiches or stir-fries. The best pulses for sprouting are:

- All types of dry peas
- Adzuki beans
- Chickpeas
- All colours of lentils

Sprouted pulses are best eaten as fresh as possible, so keep an ongoing supply coming to enjoy them daily.

To sprout pulses, you'll find several types of sprouters online or in your local health food store. Or you can simply use a large mason jar with a screen lid or cheesecloth secured over the top with an elastic band. Good rinsing and drainage are essential, so you will need to give your sprouts a thorough rinse two to three times daily and then give them a shake to get rid of as much water as possible.

When ready, lentil sprouts are about ½ to 1 inch (1.25 to 2.5 cm) long and peas, adzuki beans and chickpeas 1 to 2 inches (2.5 to 5 cm).

To grow your own pulse sprouts:

1. Check your pulses to ensure you have removed any discoloured or broken ones that could go mouldy, along with any debris.
2. Soak in lukewarm water to wake up your dormant dry seeds and set off the sprouting process. Cover the seeds with at least three times as much water as seed (and it doesn't hurt to add extra water). Stir the water to ensure all the seeds have even contact with it and leave them to soak overnight (or for 12 hours).
3. Skim off any seeds or debris floating on the water.
4. Before you end the soak, the pulses should be a little paler and swollen; allow more soaking time if they still look dark. If just a few odd pulses appear hard and dark, discard those into the compost.

5. Place your well-soaked pulses into a sprouter or sterile mason jar with a screen lid or cheesecloth secured over the top with an elastic band.

6. Rinsing is critical in growing healthy and delicious sprouts. Use cool water and a lot of it to give the sprouts a thorough rinse over the sink. (You can catch this water in a pot or bin to dump into your garden.) Rinse two to three times daily.

7. Drain as much of the water from your sprouts as possible; shake it upside down and be diligent about not leaving moisture to pool in your sprouter.

8. Store your sprouter on an airy counter or any place where there is good circulation. If the weather is hot and humid, placing it near a fan works well.

9. When your sprouts are ready to eat (usually after four to five days, or after they've sprouted tiny leaves), give them a final rinse and shake them vigorously. Leave them in the open air for a few more hours to dry further before storing in the refrigerator. The dryer they are, the better they will keep. Whizzing them in a salad spinner or swinging them around in an absorbent cloth bag or tea towel is a good way to shake the water off those sprouts.

10. Once the sprouts are as dry as you can get them, store in a sealed container or produce bag in the refrigerator. If you are concerned that the sprouts are still too damp, tuck in some paper towel or a clean cloth to sponge up moisture, or punch a few air holes into a plastic bag and use that for storage. Kept cold, your sprouts should last for several days, but as they are best eaten as soon as possible, keep them coming and eat lots daily!

Warning: Do not sprout kidney beans for eating, as they contain high levels of phytohemagglutinin (PHA). This toxin is easily removed by appropriate cooking; see Pulse Soaking and Cooking Times (page 101). While kidney beans are safe and healthy when properly cooked, it is not recommended they be eaten as raw sprouts. Although other pulses also contain PHA, the quantities are small enough that they can be safely eaten as sprouts.

Another fresh option for your pulses is to snip off fresh pea and fava shoots and toss into salads and stir-fries. You can either sacrifice a few early garden shoots, or grow in a small pot on a sunny windowsill.

Maple-baked Northern Beans

SERVES 6

Whether you enjoy them on their own, with creamy polenta or piled on toast beneath a runny egg, baked beans are nourishing and comforting. For a quick and hearty breakfast, prepare a day ahead and reheat in the oven. *Vegan* WITH VEGAN WORCESTERSHIRE SAUCE

1 medium yellow onion

4 whole cloves

2½ cups (600 mL) dry navy beans, soaked in water overnight

6 Tbsp (90 mL) maple syrup

¼ cup (60 mL) unsulphured molasses

2 tsp (10 mL) dry mustard powder

1 clove garlic, minced

2 Tbsp (30 mL) tomato paste

2 tsp (10 mL) Worcestershire sauce

1 tsp (5 mL) baking soda

4 cups (1 L) boiling water

1 Tbsp (15 mL) apple cider vinegar

Salt and pepper, to taste

Preheat oven to 250F (121C).

Peel the onion, trim its ends and stud it with the cloves.

To cook in the oven, place onion in a 4-quart (16-cup/3.8-L) Dutch oven along with all other ingredients except for vinegar, salt and pepper. Cover pot and place in the oven. Lifting the lid and stirring occasionally, cook the beans for 6 to 7 hours, until they are tender and the liquid has reduced to a thick glaze.

To cook in a slow cooker, boil beans in a medium pot for 10 to 12 minutes. Drain and add to slow cooker along with all other ingredients except for vinegar, salt and pepper. Cook on low for 6 hours, or until they are tender and the liquid has reduced to a thick glaze.

Add vinegar and season to taste with salt and pepper. Remove onion and serve.

Broad Bean Succotash with Ricotta and Poached Eggs on Toast

SERVES 6

In the heart of summer when broad beans, corn, tomatoes and basil are at their peak, linger over this brunch dish on a sunny patio.

3 cups (710 mL) shelled broad beans
1 Tbsp (15 mL) olive oil
1 Tbsp (15 mL) butter
1 leek, rinsed and thinly sliced
1 clove garlic, minced
3 cups (710 mL) fresh corn kernels
2 cups (475 mL) halved
   cherry tomatoes

2 Tbsp (30 mL) julienned basil leaves
Salt and pepper to taste
3 Tbsp (45 mL) white vinegar
6 large eggs
Rustic loaf, sliced
½ cup (120 mL) fresh ricotta

In a pot of boiling salted water, cook beans until tender, about 3 minutes. Drain, then immediately immerse in ice water to stop the cooking process. Once beans are cool, pop inner beans from shells.

Heat oil and butter in a large skillet over medium heat. Add leek and cook until translucent and tender. Add garlic and cook 30 seconds. Add corn and cherry tomatoes, cooking until tomatoes just begin to break down, about 1 to 2 minutes. Remove from heat, add beans and basil, and season to taste with salt and pepper.

Bring a medium saucepan of water to a boil. Add vinegar and reduce to a simmer. Create a whirlpool in the water by stirring around the outer edge of the pot. One at a time, crack eggs into a small bowl and lower into hot water. Immediately use a spoon to fold egg whites back around the yolk. Cook for about 3 minutes for medium-firm eggs, or to desired consistency, and drain over kitchen towel.

While eggs are poaching, toast bread and spread with ricotta. Spoon succotash onto toast and top with poached egg.

Smoky Lentil Frittata

SERVES 6

Le Puy lentils give this egg dish an extra protein boost, while smoked Gouda adds a lovely creaminess and depth of flavour.

2 Tbsp (30 mL) butter, divided

2 medium leeks, dark green tops removed, thinly sliced

12 large eggs

½ cup (120 mL) 35 percent cream

¾ cup (180 mL) grated smoked Gouda

½ tsp (2.5 mL) salt

¼ tsp (1 mL) pepper

1 cup (250 mL) cooked Le Puy lentils (or substitute other green lentil)

1 cup (250 mL) watercress, rinsed and torn

Preheat oven to 350F (180C). Heat 1 tablespoon (15 mL) of the butter in a large non-stick pan. Sauté leeks over low heat until softened, about 5 minutes.

In a large bowl, whisk together eggs and cream. Stir in half the cheese, along with the salt and pepper.

Increase heat to medium and add remaining butter to the pan. Pour egg mixture over the leeks. Distribute lentils evenly over top, followed by watercress. Cook without stirring until the edges begin to set, about 7 minutes.

Sprinkle remaining cheese over frittata and transfer pan to oven. Bake until golden and set, about 25 minutes.

Pinto Bean Breakfast Tacos

MAKES 10 TACOS

Start your day on a spicy note with these protein-packed tacos.

VINAIGRETTE

1 dried pasilla chili (or substitute 1 canned chipotle pepper and 1 Tbsp/15 mL adobo sauce)

1 Tbsp (15 mL) apple cider vinegar

1 Tbsp (15 mL) lime juice

1 tsp (5 mL) honey

1 Tbsp (15 mL) Dijon mustard

¼ cup (60 mL) + 2 Tbsp (30 mL) olive oil, divided

Salt and pepper, to taste

1 medium onion, diced small

2 cloves garlic, minced

4 cups (1 L) cooked pinto beans

10 eggs

10 small corn tortillas

½ cup (120 mL) crumbled queso fresco or feta

¼ cup (60 mL) roughly chopped cilantro

Avocado, for garnish

In a frying pan over medium-high heat, toast chili until fragrant, about 3 minutes. In a bowl, cover chili with boiling water. Cover with plastic wrap and let stand until softened, about 30 minutes. (Skip this step if using a canned chipotle pepper.)

In a food processor or high-powered blender, combine chili with 2 tablespoons (30 mL) water from the soaking liquid. Add vinegar, lime juice, honey and mustard. Purée until smooth. With the machine running, slowly drizzle ¼ cup (60 mL) of the oil through the feed tube to emulsify. Season to taste with salt and pepper.

Heat remaining 2 Tbsp (30 mL) oil in a large skillet. Add onion and cook over medium heat until soft and translucent. Add garlic and cook until fragrant, about 30 seconds. Add beans and cook until warmed through. Add chili vinaigrette and stir to incorporate.

In a skillet over medium heat, fry eggs until just set. Warm corn tortillas in a microwave for 45 seconds. Fill tortillas with bean mixture, top with egg and garnish with queso fresco, cilantro and avocado.

Socca Tart with Olive Tapenade

SERVES 6 AS AN APPETIZER

Socca is a traditional chickpea flour flatbread originating in Genoa, and is popular in southern France. This version is also popular whenever it's served, especially with this savoury olive tapenade.

BATTER

2 ¾ cups (650 mL) chickpea flour

1 tsp (5 mL) salt

½ Tbsp (7.5 mL) cumin

1 cup (250 mL) water

2 Tbsp (30 mL) canola oil, divided

TAPENADE

1 clove garlic

1 rounded Tbsp (20 mL) capers

⅓ cup (80 mL) Niçoise olives, pitted (or substitute Kalamata olives)

⅓ cup (80 mL) Cerignola olives, pitted (or substitute another green olive)

Small bunch parsley

¼ cup (60 mL) feta

Juice of half lemon

⅓ cup (80 mL) extra-virgin olive oil

Pea shoots or baby greens, for garnish

In a medium bowl, whisk together chickpea flour, salt, cumin, water and 1 tablespoon (15 mL) of the canola oil. Rest the batter for 1 hour at room temperature.

In the bowl of a food processor, combine all tapenade ingredients except olive oil and garnish. Pulse mixture to coarsely chop. Pour olive oil through the top of the machine and pulse the mixture until just combined. Place in a flat dish and set aside.

Fifteen minutes before baking, preheat oven to 450F (230C). Place remaining tablespoon (15 mL) canola oil on a large baking sheet and preheat pan until oil is hot, about 5 minutes. With a spatula, carefully add a ¼-inch (0.6-cm) layer of batter to the baking sheet, tilting the sheet so that the batter covers the entire surface. Cook just until the sides and middle begin to colour, about 2 minutes.

Flip socca onto cutting board. Slice and serve warm topped with tapenade. Garnish with pea shoots or baby greens.

Sweet Pea and Halloumi Fritters

MAKES 10 TO 12 FRITTERS

These crispy, savoury fritters showcase fresh English peas when they're at their sweet, perfectly ripe peak. Aromatic leeks and shallots, bright parsley, coriander and dill, and salty halloumi cheese contrast with the sweet peas beautifully.

2 large leeks, dark green tops removed

3 Tbsp (45 mL) olive oil

½ cup (120 mL) finely chopped shallots

2 cups (475 mL) shelled English peas

½ cup (120 mL) chopped flatleaf parsley

1 Tbsp (15 mL) finely chopped fresh dill

¾ tsp (4 mL) ground coriander seed

Salt and pepper to taste

½ cup (120 mL) all-purpose flour

2 tsp (10 mL) baking powder

½ tsp (2.5 mL) salt

1 egg

⅓ cup (80 mL) 3.5 percent milk, at room temperature

3 Tbsp (45 mL) butter, melted

8 oz (225 g) halloumi cheese, diced small

½ cup (120 mL) canola oil

Crème fraîche, to serve

Halved lemons, to serve

Slice leeks into ½-inch (1.25-cm) rounds and rinse well in a colander to remove any dirt.

Heat olive oil in a large sauté pan over medium heat. Add the leeks and shallots. Cook, stirring occasionally, until softened, about 10 minutes.

Add peas, parsley, dill and coriander to the leek mixture. Cook for 5 minutes, smashing with a wooden spoon or potato masher until about one third of the peas are mashed. Season with salt and pepper to taste.

In a large bowl, whisk together the flour, baking powder, ½ tsp (5 mL) salt, egg, milk and butter. Fold the vegetable mixture and diced halloumi into the batter until just combined.

In a deep fryer or deep saucepan, heat canola oil over medium heat until it registers 350F (180C) on a thermometer. Working with a quarter of the batter per batch, divide into about three large fritters and fry until golden brown and crisp, approximately 2 to 3 minutes per side. Transfer to a plate lined with paper towels and keep warm. Repeat process with remaining batter.

Serve fritters immediately with crème fraîche and lemon halves.

Crispy Chickpeas

MAKES APPROXIMATELY 6 CUPS (1.4 L)

Delicious eaten on their own or tossed onto salads and soups in lieu of croutons, these roasted chickpeas will be requested often and devoured quickly.

I lb (455 g) dry chickpeas

I cup + ¼ cup (250 + 60 mL) red wine vinegar, divided

I tsp (5 mL) Dijon mustard

2 tsp (10 mL) cumin

I tsp (5 mL) ground coriander

I½ tsp (7.5 mL) salt

¼ tsp (I mL) pepper

2 Tbsp (30 mL) olive oil

Place chickpeas in a medium bowl. Add 1 cup (250 mL) red wine vinegar and enough cold water to cover by 1 inch (2.5 cm). Soak overnight, drain and rinse. Bring 9 cups (2.1 L) water to the boil; add chickpeas and simmer for 1 hour and 30 minutes, or until just tender.

Preheat oven to 350F (180C).

Drain chickpeas. In a small bowl, combine remaining ¼ cup (60 mL) vinegar, along with mustard, cumin, ground coriander, salt and pepper. Whisk in oil to emulsify.

Toss chickpeas in dressing and spread evenly over a parchment-lined baking sheet. Roast, stirring occasionally, until chickpeas are dark golden in colour, about 35 minutes. Once completely cool, chickpeas can be stored in an airtight container for up to 1 week.

Chickpea Flavours

Crispy chickpeas lend themselves to a variety of flavour combinations. Try our suggestions below and experiment with your own! Follow the instructions on page 116, substituting the following seasoning combinations:

MAPLE CINNAMON

1 Tbsp (15 mL) pure maple syrup

½ tsp (2.5 mL) cinnamon

2 Tbsp (30 mL) raw sugar

1 tsp (5 mL) salt

ZAATAR

½ Tbsp (7.5 mL) sumac

½ Tbsp (7.5 mL) thyme

½ Tbsp (7.5 mL) sesame seeds

½ Tbsp (7.5 mL) salt

CHEESY GARLIC

2 cloves garlic, minced

1 tsp (5 mL) salt

½ cup (120 mL) Parmigiano-Reggiano

Butter Bean Croquettes

MAKES ABOUT 2 DOZEN

Served hot and crispy with a squeeze of lemon juice, these creamy croquettes are delightful bites.

2 Tbsp (30 mL) olive oil

I shallot, minced

2 cloves garlic, minced

3 cups (710 mL) cooked butter beans (or substitute lima beans)

I Tbsp (15 mL) finely chopped fresh oregano

I Tbsp (15 mL) finely chopped fresh parsley

Zest and juice of half lemon

Salt and pepper, to taste

½ cup (120 mL) finely grated Parmigiano-Reggiano

¾ cup (180 mL) all-purpose flour

I egg, beaten

I cup (250 mL) bread crumbs

¼ cup (60 mL) vegetable oil

Lemon halves, wrapped in cheesecloth

Heat olive oil in a skillet over medium heat. Cook shallot until soft and translucent. Add garlic and cook until fragrant, about 30 seconds. Add beans and cook until soft and warmed through. Add herbs and lemon juice; season to taste with salt and pepper.

Remove bean mixture from heat and allow to cool to room temperature. Add cheese and mash with the back of a fork or potato masher just until beans begin to break down. Allow mixture to firm up in the fridge for 1 hour.

Roll bean mixture into small balls then into short cylinders. Place the flour, beaten egg and bread crumbs into three separate bowls. Season each with a little salt and pepper. Roll croquettes in flour, then coat with egg and bread crumbs.

In a large skillet, heat vegetable oil over medium-high heat until hot. Fry croquettes in batches until golden brown. Serve immediately with lemon halves. Croquettes can also be made ahead and reheated in a 375F (190C) oven. Squeeze lemon juice on individual croquettes just before eating.

Lentil and Mushroom Pâté

MAKES ABOUT 2 CUPS (275 ML)

Brown lentils and crimini mushrooms form the base of this densely flavoured pâté, which will be devoured by vegetarians and meat-eaters alike when served on a cheese board at cocktail hour.

½ cup (120 mL) brown lentils, rinsed and picked over

1 cup (250 mL) water

1 bay leaf

1 sprig fresh thyme

2 Tbsp (30 mL) butter

1 Tbsp (15 mL) olive oil

2 shallots, finely chopped

2 cloves garlic, minced

2 cups (475 mL) thinly sliced crimini mushrooms

1 Tbsp (15 mL) Madeira wine

Pinch of allspice

3 Tbsp (45 mL) 35 percent cream

Salt and pepper to taste

In a pot over high heat, bring lentils and water to a boil. Add bay leaf and thyme and reduce to a simmer; cover and cook until lentils are tender and water has been absorbed, about 20 minutes. Remove from heat and let stand.

Combine butter and oil in a sauté pan over medium heat. Add shallots and cook until soft and translucent; add garlic and cook for an additional 30 seconds. Add mushrooms and cook until soft. Remove from pan and deglaze with Madeira wine.

In a food processor or high-powered blender, combine lentils, mushroom mixture and allspice. With the motor running, add cream and season to taste with salt and pepper. Chill in the refrigerator for at least 2 hours before serving.

Crispy Green Beans with Horseradish Cream

SERVES 8

Serve these tempura-style beans at happy hour and they will vanish almost instantly.

HORSERADISH CREAM
1 Tbsp (15 mL) apple cider vinegar
½ tsp (2.5 mL) salt
¼ tsp (1 mL) pepper
2 tsp (10 mL) honey
2 tsp (10 mL) Dijon mustard
2-inch (5-cm) piece
    horseradish, peeled
½ cup (120 mL) sour cream

BEANS
1½ lbs (680 g) green beans, trimmed
4 egg whites
2 cups (475 mL) flour
2½ cups (600 mL) club soda
Vegetable oil for frying
Salt to taste

In a small bowl, combine vinegar, salt, pepper, honey and mustard. Grate horseradish using a Microplane and add to vinegar mixture. Stir in sour cream and adjust seasoning if desired.

Bring a large pot of salted water to a boil. Blanch beans for 1 minute and immediately immerse in a bowl of ice water. Drain, pat dry and set aside.

In a large bowl using an electric mixer, beat egg whites until soft peaks form. Whisk in flour and club soda. Chill in the refrigerator until cold, about 1 hour.

Heat 3 inches (7.5 cm) of vegetable oil in a large pot or deep fryer until it reaches 350F (180C) on a thermometer. Place all of the beans into batter, then working with one at a time, shake off excess batter and drop into oil. Fry in small batches until golden brown, about 2 minutes. Carefully remove, drain on paper towel and season with salt.

Serve hot with horseradish cream.

Butter Bean Relish

MAKES ABOUT 6 CUPS (1.4 L)

Add a kick to veggie burgers with this spicy, vinegary condiment.

3 cups (710 mL) fresh butter beans

6 cups (1.4 L) apple cider vinegar

1 Tbsp (15 mL) brown sugar

2 Tbsp (30 mL) salt

1 Tbsp (15 mL) yellow mustard seeds

1½ tsp (7.5 mL) celery seeds

1 Tbsp (15 mL) turmeric

1 tsp (5 mL) red pepper flakes

1 medium onion, diced small

2 red bell peppers, diced small

1 jalapeno, minced

1 small head green cabbage, finely chopped

3 green tomatoes

½ Tbsp (7.5 mL) yellow mustard

Bring a large pot of water to a boil. Add beans and cook 4 minutes. Drain beans and allow to cool.

Combine vinegar, brown sugar and salt in a small pot and bring to a boil over high heat. Reduce heat to simmer and cook until reduced by half, about 20 minutes.

Add mustard seeds, celery seeds, turmeric, red pepper flakes, onion, bell peppers, jalapeno, cabbage and tomatoes to reduced mixture and cook over medium heat until the cabbage has softened, about 10 minutes. Add butter beans and mustard and allow mixture to cool.

Allow mixture to set for 6 hours in the refrigerator before serving.

Red Lentil Condiment

MAKES ABOUT 2 CUPS (475 ML)

This spread is wonderful on sandwiches, tossed with pasta or served as an antipasto with cheese and crackers.

¾ cup (180 mL) dry red lentils, rinsed and picked over

1½ cups (350 mL) Classic Garlic Broth, recipe on page 145 (or other vegetable stock)

2 Tbsp (30 mL) olive oil

1 cup (250 mL) diced fennel

¾ cup (180 mL) diced roasted red peppers

Half medium white onion, diced

½ cup (120 mL) diced artichoke hearts

⅓ cup (80 mL) diced green olives

½ cup (120 mL) diced crimini mushrooms

3 cloves garlic, minced

¼ tsp (1 mL) cayenne pepper

½ tsp (2.5 mL) smoked paprika

2 Tbsp (30 mL) sherry vinegar (or other wine vinegar)

1 Tbsp (15 mL) minced flatleaf parsley

Salt and pepper to taste

Place lentils, stock and a pinch of salt in a medium pot and bring to a boil. Cover, reduce heat to a simmer and cook until al dente, about 10 minutes.

In a large pot, heat olive oil over medium heat. Add fennel, peppers, onion, artichoke, olives, mushrooms and garlic. Cook until vegetables are slightly softened, about 5 minutes. Add cayenne and paprika and sauté until spices are cooked and fragrant, about 1 minute. Fold in red lentils, vinegar and parsley. Season to taste with salt and pepper. Can be served warm or cold. Stores in the refrigerator for up to one week.

Cannellini Bean and Caramelized Onion Dip

MAKES ABOUT 3 CUPS (710 ML)

Creamy cannellini beans and sweet caramelized onions form the base of this flavour-dense dip that is wonderful served alongside crudité and crostini.

2 Tbsp (30 mL) butter

1 Tbsp (15 mL) olive oil

3 medium yellow onions, sliced into thin rounds

3 Tbsp (45 mL) red wine vinegar

1 cup (250 mL) sour cream

1 cup (250 mL) cream cheese, softened

1 cup (250 mL) cooked cannellini beans

Juice of half lemon

1 Tbsp (15 mL) finely chopped flatleaf parsley

1 tsp (5 mL) finely chopped fresh thyme

Salt and pepper to taste

Combine butter and oil in a large sauté pan. Add onions and cook over low heat until soft and caramelized, about 35 minutes. Add red wine vinegar and cook until vinegar is reduced by half. Remove from heat and cool to room temperature.

In the bowl of a food processor, blend sour cream and cream cheese until smooth. Add beans, cooled onions, lemon juice, parsley and thyme. Pulse the mixture lightly to retain some texture. Season to taste with salt and pepper.

Following spread, clockwise from top left: Cannellini Bean and Caramelized Onion Dip, Red Lentil Condiment (page 122) and Miso and Charred Scallion Hummus (page 126).

Miso and Charred Scallion Hummus

MAKES ABOUT 2 CUPS (475 ML)

Our Japanese-inspired twist on traditional hummus gets its deep "umami" flavour from white (shiro) miso. A fermented soybean product that is high in protein, vitamins and minerals, miso is available in paste form and is a wonderful addition to marinades and sauces.

3 whole scallions, root
   ends discarded

2 cups (475 mL) cooked chickpeas

1 clove garlic, minced

1 Tbsp (15 mL) tahini

1 Tbsp (15 mL) white (shiro) miso

1 Tbsp (15 mL) rice vinegar

1 Tbsp (15 mL) lemon juice

½ tsp (2.5 mL) cumin

3 Tbsp (45 mL) olive oil

Salt to taste

In a hot grill pan or on the barbecue, cook whole dry scallions on all sides until outer layers are charred. Set aside.

In the bowl of a food processor, blend chickpeas, garlic and tahini until smooth. Add miso, vinegar, lemon juice and cumin. With the food processor running, slowly stream olive oil through the opening at the top. Season hummus to taste with salt and transfer to a bowl. Finely chop charred scallions and stir through hummus.

Quick Pickled Beans

MAKES 1 LB (455 G) PICKLED BEANS

Whether you toss one in a Caesar or pile a few on a cheese board, there's nothing like the vinegary snap of a pickled bean.

1 lb (455 g) green beans, stems removed

1½ cups (350 mL) water

1¼ cups (300 mL) white wine vinegar

4 Tbsp (60 mL) sugar

1 Tbsp (15 mL) pickling salt

2 tsp (10 mL) mustard seeds

¼ tsp (1 mL) red pepper flakes

2 cloves garlic, sliced

4 sprigs dill

Bring a large pot of salted water to a boil. Prepare a large bowl of ice water. Add green beans to boiling water and cook until al dente, about 2 minutes. Drain and immediately plunge into ice water. Once completely cool, drain.

In a small saucepan, bring water, vinegar, sugar, salt, mustard seeds, red pepper flakes and garlic to a boil. Remove from heat and stir to ensure sugar has dissolved. Cool completely.

Stand blanched beans in mason jars and add dill sprigs. Fill jars with cooled pickling liquid and allow to infuse for a minimum of 6 hours before eating; the flavour will become stronger over time. Will keep in the fridge for 2 weeks.

Crispy Chickpea Power Bowl with Tahini Dressing

SERVES 4

Brimming with nutrient-dense ingredients and bold flavours, this hearty salad is a meal in itself. The cumin- and coriander-roasted crispy chickpeas are a welcome departure from traditional croutons.

FARRO AND YAMS

3 cups (710 mL) water

½ tsp (2.5 mL) salt, plus more for yam

2 Tbsp (30 mL) olive oil, divided

1 cup (250 mL) farro, rinsed

1 large yam, peeled and chopped into large dice

Pepper

TAHINI DRESSING

¼ cup (60 mL) tahini

⅓ cup (80 mL) apple cider vinegar

¼ cup (60 mL) nutritional yeast flakes

¼ cup (60 mL) soy sauce

½ cup (120 mL) water, plus more if needed

1 tsp (5 mL) sumac

1 tsp (5 mL) thyme

1 tsp (5 mL) sesame seeds

1 clove garlic

¾ cup (180 mL) vegetable oil

Salt and pepper to taste

GREENS AND CHICKPEAS

4 cups (1 L) fresh spinach

1 large beet, shredded or spiralized

1 cucumber, sliced in ¼-inch (0.6-cm) rounds

2 cups (475 mL) crispy chickpeas, recipe on page 116

2 Tbsp (30 mL) roughly chopped flatleaf parsley

1 Tbsp (15 mL) roughly chopped mint

Bring water to a rolling boil. Add salt, 1 tablespoon (15 mL) oil and farro. Reduce heat to a simmer, then cover and cook until tender, about 30 minutes. Remove from heat and allow to cool with lid on.

Continued on page 132

CRISPY CHICKPEA POWER BOWL WITH TAHINI DRESSING CONTINUED

While farro is cooling, preheat oven to 375F (190C). Toss yam with remaining tablespoon (15 mL) oil and season with salt and pepper. Roast until soft and caramelized, about 30 minutes.

In a food processor or high-powered blender, blend all dressing ingredients except oil, salt and pepper. With the machine running, slowly drizzle oil through the feed tube to emulsify. Adjust consistency as desired with additional water. Season to taste with salt and pepper.

Divide farro, yams, spinach, beet, cucumber and chickpeas among 4 bowls, arranging ingredients into clusters for visual impact. Top with dressing and garnish with herbs.

Dan's Endless Salad Bowl

Combine beans, shoots and sprouted pulses with your favourite greens and herbs to create an endless array of fresh, protein-packed salads that show off the complex flavours of your homegrown pulse varieties. Just select from the options for dressings, pulses, herbs and greens depending on what's seasonal and available.

DRESSING

Olive oil and lemon juice (or wine vinegar)

Ruckle Salad Dressing (see sidebar)

Salt and pepper

PULSES

Sprouted chickpeas or lentils (see Sprouting Pulses, Boosting Health, page 103)

Pea or fava shoots (see page 105)

Mix of your favourite precooked beans, at room temperature

GREENS

Lettuce

Kale

Spinach

Arugula

Chicory

Endive

Radicchio

HERBS AND AROMATICS

Leeks

Shallots

Chives

Garlic

Garlic scapes

Dill

Basil

Parsley

Ruckle Salad Dressing

Soak **1 cup (250 mL) Ruckle beans** overnight, bring to the boil in 3 times their volume of water and simmer 50 minutes or until tender. Drain and purée in a food processor or blender, adding a little of the cooking liquid until smooth. Blend in **2 Tbsp (30 mL) olive oil, 1 Tbsp (30 mL) wine vinegar, 2 Tbsp (30 mL) fresh parsley, 1 Tbsp (15 mL) chives** and **2 Tbsp (30 mL) fresh basil**. Allow to cool to room temperature before serving over salad.

Picnic Bean Salad with Poppy-seed Dressing

SERVES 6 TO 10

No picnic is complete without a robust salad that will stand up to transport, and this update on traditional bean salad is sure to become your family's standby. *Vegan* IF SUGAR OR MAPLE SYRUP IS SUBSTITUTED FOR HONEY

POPPY-SEED DRESSING

½ cup + 1 Tbsp (120 mL + 15 mL) olive oil, divided

1 shallot, minced

1 Tbsp (15 mL) honey

3 Tbsp (45 mL) apple cider vinegar

1 Tbsp (15 mL) Dijon mustard

Salt and pepper to taste

2 tsp (10 mL) poppy seeds

SALAD

2 cups (475 mL) snow peas, side strings removed (or substitute sugar snap peas)

1 cup (250 mL) shelled and cooked green peas

2 cups (475 mL) green beans, tips removed, cut in half and blanched

1 cup (250 mL) cooked chickpeas

1 cup (250 mL) cooked navy beans

1 cup (250 mL) cooked kidney beans

3 Tbsp (45 mL) flatleaf parsley

In a pan over medium heat, sauté shallot in 1 tablespoon (15 mL) of the oil until soft and translucent. Remove from heat and allow to cool.

In a food processor or high-powered blender, combine cooled shallots, honey, vinegar and mustard. With the machine running, slowly drizzle remaning oil through the feed tube to emulsify. Season to taste with salt and pepper. Transfer to a bowl and stir in poppy seeds.

Combine pulses and parsley in a large bowl and toss with dressing.

Lentil and Butternut Squash Salad with Kale, Blue Cheese and Roasted Grapes

SERVES 6 TO 8

Earthy and hearty, this warm salad is especially lovely in cooler months. For a particularly beautiful presentation, layer the ingredients on a large platter. *Vegan* IF YOU SKIP THE BLUE CHEESE

I small butternut squash, cut into medium dice

I Tbsp (I5 mL) olive oil

Salt and pepper

I½ cups (350 mL) black lentils, rinsed and picked through

3 cups (7I0 mL) water

I Tbsp (I5 mL) butter or oil

I sprig thyme

I½ cups (350 mL) red seedless grapes, halved

I0 cups (2.4 L) torn kale leaves, rinsed

¼ cup (60 mL) crumbled blue cheese

VINAIGRETTE

I shallot, minced

I clove garlic

I Tbsp (I5 mL) Dijon mustard

3 Tbsp (45 mL) red wine vinegar

½ cup (I20 mL) olive oil

Salt and pepper to taste

Preheat oven to 375F (190C).

In a medium bowl, toss butternut squash with olive oil and season with salt and pepper. Roast on a baking sheet until squash is tender and caramelized, about 35 minutes.

Combine lentils, water, butter and thyme in a medium pot. Bring to a rapid boil then reduce to a gentle simmer. Cover and cook until tender, 20 to 30 minutes. Remove from heat, season with salt and allow to sit covered until cool.

In a 200F (95C) oven, bake grapes on a parchment-lined baking sheet until they've shrunk by half, about 40 minutes.

Continued on page 138

LENTIL AND BUTTERNUT SQUASH SALAD WITH KALE, BLUE CHEESE AND ROASTED GRAPE CONTINUED

In a food processor or high-powered blender, combine shallot, garlic, mustard and vinegar. With the machine running, slowly drizzle oil through the feed tube to emulsify. Season to taste with salt and pepper.

In a large bowl, massage kale leaves by hand with 3 Tbsp (45 mL) of the vinaigrette. Spread kale on a platter. Layer with lentils, squash, grapes and blue cheese. Drizzle with remaining vinaigrette.

Spring Shoot Salad with Glorious Green Dressing

SERVES 4 TO 6

From the pea shoots, fava beans and herbs to the creamy avocado dressing, this simple tossed salad is vibrantly green and bursting with fresh flavours. *Vegan* IF YOU SKIP THE FETA

2 cups (475 mL) fresh fava beans

3 cups (710 mL) pea shoots

8 cups (1.9 L) mixed greens

¼ cup (60 mL) slivered almonds

¼ cup (60 mL) crumbled feta

GLORIOUS GREEN DRESSING

half avocado, halved and pitted

¼ cup (60 mL) flatleaf parsley, stems removed

Juice of 1 lime

½ cup (120 mL) water

1 clove garlic

1 Tbsp (15 mL) honey or sugar

¼ cup (60 mL) olive oil

Salt and pepper to taste

Bring a pot of salted water to a rolling boil. Prepare a bowl of ice water. Blanch fava beans for 2 minutes, then drain and plunge into ice water. Pop inner beans out of shells, if desired.

Scoop avocado halves into a food processor or high-powered blender. Add parsley, lime juice, water, garlic and honey. With the machine running, slowly drizzle oil through the feed tube to emulsify. Season to taste with salt and pepper.

Toss pea shoots and greens with dressing. Top with fava beans, almonds and feta cheese.

Farmstand Minestrone Soup with Basil Pistou

SERVES 6 TO 8

This nourishing soup is wonderful any time of year, and the fresh ingredients can be adjusted according to what is in season where you live. A drizzle of fresh basil pistou atop each serving adds vibrant flavour.

2 Tbsp (30 mL) olive oil

I onion, diced

I leek, dark green tops removed

2 carrots, peeled and diced

2 stalks celery, diced

4 cloves garlic, minced

½ tsp (2.5 mL) crushed red
   pepper flakes

¼ cup (60 mL) white wine

2 Tbsp (30 mL) tomato paste

28-oz (796-mL) can
   crushed tomatoes

3 sprigs oregano

2 bay leaves

Parmigiano-Reggiano rind
   (about 2 oz/60 g)

6 cups (1.4 L) water

2 large Yukon Gold potatoes, peeled
   and cut into ½-inch (1.25-cm) pieces

1½ cups (350 mL) cooked
   cannellini beans

1½ cups (350 mL) cooked
   kidney beans

3 oz (80 g) small shell pasta

⅓ cup (80 mL) peas

I small zucchini, diced

Salt and pepper, to taste

BASIL PISTOU

 2 cloves garlic

I cup (250 mL) basil leaves

½ cup (120 mL) olive oil

2 Tbsp (30 mL) freshly grated
   Parmigiano-Reggiano

I tsp (5 mL) grated lemon zest

Salt to taste

Continued on page 142

FARMSTAND MINESTRONE SOUP WITH BASIL PISTOU CONTINUED

Heat oil in a large, heavy pot over medium heat. Add onion, leek, carrots, celery, garlic and red pepper flakes. Cook, stirring often, until onion is translucent and carrots are tender, about 10 minutes. Add wine and reduce liquid by half, about 1 minute. Add tomato paste and stir to coat the vegetables; cook until slightly darkened, about 3 minutes. Add crushed tomatoes, herbs, rind, water, potatoes and beans.

Bring to a boil, then reduce heat and simmer until potatoes are tender, about 15 minutes. Add pasta, peas and zucchini; cook until pasta is tender, about 5 minutes. Discard Parmesan rind and herbs.

For the pistou, pulse garlic, basil and oil in a food processor until finely chopped. Transfer to a small bowl and add cheese and lemon zest. Season to taste with salt. Top each serving of soup with a drizzle of pistou.

Pea and Sorrel Gazpacho

SERVES 6

This summer soup showcases fresh sweet peas and the leaves and stems of sorrel, a perennial herb with a bright, acidic flavour.

1 Tbsp (15 mL) extra-virgin olive oil, plus extra for garnish

2 stalks celery, cut into medium dice

1 onion, cut into medium dice

1 leek, white part only, cut into medium dice

1 clove garlic, minced

5 cups (1.2 L) Classic Garlic Broth, recipe on page 145 (or other vegetable stock)

1 lb (455 g) fresh peas, shelled

1 cup (250 mL) chopped sorrel leaves

¼ cup (60 mL) flatleaf parsley

1 Tbsp (15 mL) mint

½ cup (120 mL) 35 percent cream

Salt and white pepper to taste

Heat 1 Tbsp (15 mL) olive oil in a medium saucepan. Cook celery, onion, leek and garlic on medium-low heat until soft but not browned. Add stock and bring to a boil, then reduce heat to low. Simmer until vegetables are very tender, about 15 minutes. Allow to cool to room temperature.

Heat a large pot of salted water over high heat. Blanch peas, sorrel, parsley and mint until warmed through, about 2 minutes. Immediately transfer ingredients to a bowl of ice water to cool. Drain once cooled.

In the bowl of a blender or food processor, combine pea mixture and broth until smooth. Pass through a strainer. Stir cream through and season to taste with salt and pepper. Chill soup in the refrigerator for 1 hour before serving.

Garnish each serving with a drizzle of fruity extra-virgin olive oil.

Dan's Salt Spring Garden Soups

Soups are a great way to eat up the garden harvest, and homegrown pulses can add a flavour, texture and protein boost to your favourite garden vegetable soups. Pick from the pulse, vegetable and seasoning combinations below for enough comforting soups to see you through many a cold winter's night.

BROTH AND SEASONING OPTIONS

Classic Garlic Broth, see sidebar

Oil

Onion

Leek

Garlic

Tomato paste

Thyme

Parsley

Bay leaf

Salt and pepper to taste

Lemon juice

PULSE OPTIONS

Dry fava beans, presoaked

Kapucijner or other soup peas, presoaked

Strongly flavoured beans such as Black Coco, Black Turtle and Red Kidney, presoaked

Dry lentils, rinsed and picked through

Dry chickpeas, presoaked

VEGETABLE OPTIONS

Carrots

Celery

Potatoes

Tomatoes

Kale

Amaranth

Cabbage greens

Swiss chard

In a large pot over medium heat, heat oil and sauté onion, leek or garlic until softened. Stir in tomato paste, if using.

Add pulses, broth or water and herbs, and bring to a boil. Lower heat and simmer until tender (see Pulse Soaking and Cooking Times, page 101).

Add hard vegetables and simmer until easily pierced with a knife, about 15 minutes. Add leafy vegetables and simmer for a further 3 minutes. Remove herbs and season with salt and pepper to taste, as well as lemon juice, if using.

Classic Garlic Broth

Add **2 peeled garlic bulbs, 3 cups (710 mL) water, 1 cup (250 mL) mixed chopped vegetables, 2 sprigs parsley** and **1 bay leaf** to a medium-sized pot and bring to the boil. Simmer gently for 1 hour, then strain out solids.

Fava Bean Soup with Cilantro Pistou

SERVES 6 TO 8

A traditional peasant dish rooted in Mexican cuisine, this simple soup comes together using just a few ingredients. A cilantro-based pistou, added just before serving, adds a bright herbaceous note.

FAVA BEAN SOUP

2 pasilla chilies (or substitute
   2 canned chipotle chilies
   and 2 Tbsp/30 mL adobo sauce)

2 cups (475 mL) dry fava beans,
   soaked overnight

4 cups (1 L) water or Classic Garlic
   Broth, recipe on page 145

2 tomatoes, roughly chopped

2 cloves garlic, roughly chopped

1 yellow onion, roughly chopped

Salt and pepper

1 Tbsp (15 mL) olive oil

½ tsp (2.5 mL) saffron threads

1 tsp (5 mL) cumin

½ tsp (2.5 mL) ground coriander

CILANTRO PISTOU

1 bunch cilantro, plus extra
   for garnish

1 clove garlic

Juice of 1 lime

⅓ cup (80 mL) canola oil

Salt and pepper to taste

In a small bowl, cover chilies with 1 cup (250 mL) boiling water. Cover with cling film and allow chilies to rehydrate for about 10 minutes. (Skip rehydration step if using canned chipotle chilies.) Remove seeds and roughly chop. Reserve liquid.

Continued on page 148

FAVA BEAN SOUP WITH CILANTRO PISTOU CONTINUED

Bring fava beans, chilies, reserved liquid and 4 cups (1 L) water to a boil. Reduce heat to low and cook, covered, until tender, about 45 minutes.

Combine tomatoes, garlic, onion and a pinch of salt and pepper in the bowl of a food processor and blend until smooth.

Heat oil in a large saucepan over medium heat. Add purée and cook until it starts to thicken, about 10 minutes.

Add fava beans and cooking liquid, saffron, cumin and coriander. Cook until beans are very tender and begin to thicken the soup, about 20 minutes. Season with more salt and pepper to taste.

For the pistou, combine all ingredients in the bowl of a food processor and blend until a smooth consistency is achieved. Top each serving of soup with a generous drizzle of pistou.

Braised Peas, Broad Beans and Lettuce

SERVES 4

This dish showcases fresh produce at the peak of freshness, quickly braised with aromatics to enhance their flavours.

1 cup (250 mL) shelled English peas

1 cup (250 mL) shelled broad beans

1 Tbsp (15 mL) olive oil

1 leek, rinsed, green ends removed and thinly sliced

2 cloves garlic, minced

¾ cup (180 mL) Classic Garlic Broth, recipe on page 145 (or other vegetable stock)

3 Tbsp (45 mL) butter, softened

3 Tbsp (45 mL) flour

1 head gem lettuce, roughly chopped

1 tsp (5 mL) minced fresh thyme

Juice of half lemon

Pepper to taste

¼ cup (60 mL) large shavings Parmigiano-Reggiano, for garnish

Bring a pot of salted water to boil and prepare an ice bath. Blanch peas and beans in water for 1 minute and immediately place in cold water.

Heat oil in a sauté pan and cook leeks over medium heat until soft. Add garlic and cook until fragrant, about 30 seconds. Remove from heat.

Place stock in a small saucepan and bring to a boil. Combine butter and flour in a small bowl and whisk mixture into the hot stock. Add peas, beans, leeks, garlic and lettuce. Stir in thyme and lemon juice and season with pepper. Simmer until lettuce is wilted, about 2 minutes. Garnish with shavings of Parmigiano-Reggiano.

Haricots Verts Casserole with Crispy Shallots

SERVES 6 TO 8

Made with fresh beans, this dish puts a vibrant spin on the ubiquitous green bean casserole of the 1950s. Crispy shallots provide the perfect contrast to the creamy beans.

CRISPY SHALLOTS

2 cups (475 mL) vegetable oil

6 shallots, sliced thin on a mandolin and rings separated

¾ cup (180 mL) flour

Salt to taste

GREEN BEANS

1½ lbs (680 g) green beans, trimmed and halved

¼ cup (60 mL) butter

1 lb (455 g) mixed mushrooms, roughly chopped

1 clove garlic, minced

¼ cup (60 mL) flour

1 cup (250 mL) Classic Garlic Broth, recipe on page 145 (or other vegetable stock)

1 cup (250 mL) 10 percent cream

3 Tbsp (45 mL) Madeira wine

Pinch of nutmeg

¼ cup (60 mL) grated Parmigiano-Reggiano

Salt and pepper to taste

Preheat oven to 400F (205C).

In a large pot or deep fryer, heat oil over medium heat. Line a baking sheet with paper towel. Test oil temperature by sprinkling a pinch of flour; the oil is ready when it bubbles vigorously. In a large bowl, toss together shallots and flour. Shake off excess flour and fry shallots in batches until golden, about 3 minutes. If shallots brown too quickly, lower temperature. Carefully remove shallots from oil, drain on paper towel and season with salt.

Season a large pot of water with salt and bring to a boil. Cook beans until just tender and plunge immediately into a bowl of ice water to stop the cooking process.

In a large saucepan, dry-sauté mushrooms over medium heat until liquids have evaporated. Add butter to pan and briefly sauté mushrooms in butter until tender. Add garlic and cook 30 seconds. Add flour and stir until incorporated, 1 minute. Whisking constantly, add stock, cream, Madeira and nutmeg. Cook until the mixture has reduced, about 5 minutes. Stir in cheese and season with salt and pepper.

Add green beans to sauce and stir to coat. Transfer to a baking dish and bake until bubbling, about 12 minutes. Top with fried shallots and serve.

Dan's Sweet and Sour Lentils

SERVES 4

The recipe for this savoury mix of sweetness and spice has been much requested by friends. *Vegan* IF MOLASSES OR SUGAR IS USED

2 cups (475 mL) Classic Garlic Broth, recipe on page 145 (or other vegetable stock)

1 bay leaf

1 cup (250 mL) dry lentils, rinsed and picked over

1 clove garlic, finely chopped

⅛ tsp (0.6 mL) ground cloves

⅛ tsp (0.6 mL) nutmeg

3 Tbsp (45 mL) olive or safflower oil

3 Tbsp (45 mL) apple cider or juice

3 Tbsp (45 mL) cider vinegar

3 Tbsp (45 mL) honey, molasses or sugar

Salt to taste

Bring the stock to a boil in a large pot and add the bay leaf and lentils. Cover and simmer gently for 30 minutes, or until lentils are al dente.

Drain lentils and add the remaining ingredients. Stir to mix well. Add salt to taste. Cook for 5 more minutes, or until lentils are tender. Remove bay leaf.

Almond Pesto Pole Beans with Sourdough Crumb

This spin on the classic green bean almondine is nourishing, comforting and utterly delicious.

SOURDOUGH CRUMB

1½ cups (350 mL) large cubes of stale sourdough bread
¼ cup (60 mL) olive oil
Salt and pepper

PESTO POLE BEANS

1 clove garlic
½ cup (120 mL) flatleaf parsley, stems removed
½ cup (120 mL) basil leaves
⅓ cup (80 mL) blanched almonds
Juice of half lemon
½ tsp (2.5 mL) salt
½ cup (120 mL) grated Parmigiano-Reggiano
⅓ cup + 1 Tbsp (80 + 15 mL) olive oil, divided
2 lbs (910 g) green beans

Preheat oven to 350F (180C).

Pulse bread in a food processor until fine crumbs have formed. Mix thoroughly with oil, season with salt and pepper, spread on a baking sheet and bake until golden brown. Wipe out bowl if using for pesto.

In a food processor or high-powered blender, combine garlic, parsley and basil. Pulse to roughly chop. Add almonds, lemon juice, salt and cheese and pulse again to chop. With the machine running, slowly drizzle ⅓ cup (80 mL) of the oil through the feed tube to emulsify.

Heat the remaining 1 tablespoon (15 mL) of oil in a large skillet over medium heat. Add beans and cook until al dente, about 4 minutes.

Toss beans with pesto and transfer to a serving dish. Top with sourdough crumb.

Black Bean Burgers

MAKES 8 PATTIES

Every vegetarian has a favourite meatless burger, and this one is a great contender! Before combining the black beans with the other ingredients, roasting them in the oven enhances their flavour. When these burgers are grilled, their exterior develops a wonderful crust while the interior stays moist and chewy. The addition of chipotle chili yields a wonderful smoky flavour.

3 cups (710 mL) cooked black beans

2 Tbsp (60 mL) canola oil, plus extra for grilling

1 yellow onion, finely chopped

3 cloves garlic, minced

1 chipotle chili in adobo sauce, finely chopped

½ cup (120 mL) finely crumbled Cotija cheese (or substitute feta or queso fresco)

2 Tbsp (30 mL) mayonnaise

1 whole egg

¾ cup (180 mL) Panko bread crumbs

Pinch of salt and pepper

¼ cup (60 mL) whole pumpkin seeds

Preheat oven to 350F (180C).

Spread black beans in a single layer on a parchment-lined baking sheet. Place in oven and roast until most beans are split open and skins have dried, about 20 minutes. Remove from oven and allow to cool slightly.

Heat 2 tablespoons (30 mL) oil in a skillet over medium heat. Add onion and cook until softened, about 5 minutes. Add garlic and chipotle and cook until fragrant, about 1 minute. Transfer mixture to a large bowl.

When the beans have cooled, transfer to a food processor. Pulse until beans are roughly chopped. Transfer to the bowl with the onion mixture. Add cheese, mayonnaise, egg, Panko, salt, pepper and pumpkin seeds. Fold ingredients together until just combined. Divide mixture into 8 patties and brush the tops with canola oil.

Turn the grill to a medium-high setting, lower lid and preheat for 10 minutes. Oil the grilling grate. Place patties oil-side down and cook without moving until first side is well browned, 3 to 5 minutes. Brush tops of burgers with oil. Carefully flip and continue cooking until second side is browned, 3 to 5 minutes further. Serve burgers on buns or wrapped in lettuce with your favourite condiments.

Chickpea and Fava Falafel

SERVES 8

Whether you stuff them into pitas with Mediterranean-style accompaniments or scatter them over salads, falafel are stars in the vegetarian kitchen. In this recipe, we've followed a classic Lebanese preparation using fava beans along with chickpeas. An abundance of parsley and cilantro gives the batter a beautiful green hue and fresh flavour.

1¼ cups (300) dry fava beans, soaked overnight

1¼ cups (300) dry chickpeas, soaked overnight, divided

8 cloves garlic

1 medium yellow onion, chopped

2 Tbsp (30 mL) flour

1 tsp (5 mL) cumin

1 Tbsp (15 mL) ground coriander

1 bunch flatleaf parsley

2 bunches cilantro

3 Tbsp (45 mL) sesame seeds

1 tsp (5 mL) baking soda

Salt and pepper

Canola oil for frying

In the bowl of a food processor, blend the fava beans and half the chickpeas into a smooth paste. Add the garlic, onion, flour, cumin and coriander. Add remaining chickpeas, parsley, cilantro and sesame seeds, pulsing lightly to retain some texture. Stir in baking soda and season with salt and pepper. Allow the batter to rest in the fridge for 1 hour.

Roll the mixture into small balls, using an ice-cream scoop if desired. Heat oil in a deep pot or deep fryer until it reaches 350F (180C) on a thermometer. Fry the balls until golden brown, remove carefully and drain on paper towel.

Serve falafel immediately with accompaniments such as hummus, Greek yogurt and Harissa.

Fava Bean and Artichoke Tagliatelle

SERVES 4

Using just a few quality ingredients, this dish comes together quickly at the end of a chilly day. Buttery fava beans and the sharpness of artichokes marry perfectly in this comforting pasta dish.

1½ lbs (680 g) fresh fava beans, shelled

12 oz (340 g) tagliatelle pasta

½ cup (120 mL) butter

16 marinated artichokes, drained and halved

Zest and juice of 1 lemon

¾ cup (180 mL) grated Parmigiano-Reggiano

2 Tbsp (30 mL) coarsely chopped flatleaf parsley

Salt and pepper to taste

Bring a large pot of salted water to a rolling boil. Add fava beans and blanch for 30 seconds. Remove beans from pot, reserving water, and place in a bowl of ice water. Drain beans, peel off their skins if you prefer, and set aside.

Add pasta to the pot of reserved salted boiling water and cook to al dente, about 8 minutes. Reserve ½ cup (120 mL) of the pasta water.

Heat butter in a sauté pan over medium heat and allow milk solids to brown, about 5 minutes. Add artichokes and beans, cooking until beans are tender and artichokes are warmed through, about 4 minutes. Toss in pasta, lemon zest and juice, cheese and parsley. Add pasta water to loosen sauce and season to taste with salt and pepper.

Lentil and Mushroom Cottage Pie

When it's chilly outside and you're in need of a warming, comforting meal, this vegetarian twist on traditional cottage (or shepherd's) pie fits the bill perfectly.

LENTIL AND MUSHROOM BASE

2 Tbsp (30 mL) olive oil, divided

Half large onion, diced small

1 stalk celery, diced small

1 large carrot, diced small

2 cloves garlic, minced

1 tomato, diced

1 Tbsp (15 mL) tomato paste

1 Tbsp (15 mL) sherry

2 cups (475 mL) Classic Garlic Broth, recipe on page 145 (or other vegetable stock)

2 Tbsp (30 mL) butter

4 cups (1 L) coarsely chopped mixed mushrooms

1 cup (250 mL) dry brown lentils, rinsed and picked over

1 tsp (5 mL) coarsely chopped fresh thyme

2 Tbsp (30 mL) coarsely chopped parsley

Salt and pepper

POTATO AND PARSNIP TOPPING

Salt and pepper

3 large Yukon Gold potatoes, peeled and quartered

1 parsnip, peeled and quartered

2 Tbsp (30 mL) butter

3 Tbsp (45 mL) 3.5 percent milk

2 oz (60 g) goat cheese

Heat 1 Tbsp (15 mL) olive oil in a large pot over medium heat. Add onion, celery and carrot and cook until soft, about 5 minutes. Add garlic and cook 30 seconds. Add tomato and tomato paste and cook until the sugars begin to caramelize, about 3 minutes. Add sherry and vegetable stock; bring to a boil, then keep warm on low heat.

In a large saucepan, dry-sauté mushrooms over medium heat until liquids have evaporated. Add butter and remaining 1 Tbsp (15 mL) olive oil to pan and briefly sauté mushrooms in fat until caramelized.

Continued on page 162

LENTIL AND MUSHROOM COTTAGE PIE CONTINUED

Add mushrooms, lentils, thyme and parsley to stock base, and season mixture with salt and pepper. Cover and simmer over low heat until lentils are soft, about 30 minutes.

Put a large pot of water on to boil. Season well with salt. Cook potatoes and parsnip until a knife pierced through is easily removed. Push vegetables through a ricer (or mash with a potato masher) and combine with butter, milk and goat cheese. Season to taste with salt and pepper.

Preheat oven to 375F (180C). Transfer lentil and mushroom mixture to the bottom of a greased ovenproof dish. Top with potato and parsnip mixture and bake until golden, about 20 minutes.

Lentil Ragù

SERVES 8

When it's damp and chilly outside, a ragù served over pasta, rice or quinoa can do wonders for the soul. Le Puy lentils give this vegetarian version a hearty consistency.

2 Tbsp (30 mL) olive oil
I onion, diced small
2 peeled carrots, diced small
2 stalks celery, diced small
2 cloves garlic, minced
I cup (250 mL) red wine
28-oz (796-mL) can diced tomatoes
2 cups (475 mL) Classic Garlic Broth, recipe on page 145 (or other vegetable stock)

1½ cups (350 mL) dry Le Puy lentils, picked over and rinsed (or substitute another green or brown lentil)
2 bay leaves
2 Tbsp (30 mL) finely chopped sage
¼ cup (60 mL) finely chopped flatleaf parsley, divided
¼ cup (60 mL) 35 percent cream
¼ cup (60 mL) grated Parmigiano-Reggiano

Preheat oven to 300F (150C).

Heat olive oil in a heavy pot. Over medium heat, cook onion, carrots, celery and garlic until soft and beginning to brown, about 10 minutes.

Deglaze pan with red wine, allowing it to reduce by half. Add tomatoes, vegetables, stock and lentils. Stir in bay leaves, sage and half of the parsley.

Place uncovered pot into oven and cook until lentils have softened and liquid has reduced, about 45 minutes.

Remove bay leaves. Add remaining parsley, cream and cheese. Serve over pasta, rice, quinoa or grain of your choice.

Red Beans and Rice

SERVES 6 TO 8

A staple in Creole cuisine, this dish is simple to prepare and satisfying to eat. Boost the flavour with garnishes of fresh cilantro and Cotija cheese in addition to traditional sliced scallion. *Vegan* WITHOUT COTIJA CHEESE

¼ cup (60 mL) canola oil

8 cloves garlic, minced

6 stalks celery, diced

2 large yellow onions, diced

2 green bell peppers, diced

Salt to taste

2 tsp (10 mL) ground black pepper

1 Tbsp (15 mL) thyme

1 tsp (5 mL) oregano

1½ tsp (7.5 mL) cayenne

1 lb (455 g) dry kidney beans, soaked overnight

4 bay leaves

6 cups (1.4 L) water

1 Tbsp (15 mL) hot sauce

Cooked long-grain rice, for serving

Thinly sliced scallions, for garnish

Coarsely chopped cilantro, for garnish

Crumbled Cotija cheese, for garnish (or substitute feta or queso fresco)

Heat oil in a Dutch oven over medium-high heat. Add garlic, celery, onions and peppers and season with salt. Stirring often, cook until vegetables are soft, about 12 minutes. Add pepper, thyme, oregano and cayenne; stir until fragrant, about 2 minutes. Add beans, bay leaves and water. Bring mixture to a boil, then reduce heat to medium-low. Cook, covered, until beans are tender, about 1½ to 2 hours. Add hot sauce.

Top individual bowls of rice with bean mixture. Garnish with scallions, cilantro and Cotija cheese.

Curried Peas and Paneer

SERVES 4 TO 6

Hardy paneer cheese holds its shape in this mild curry, which brims with sweet green peas. Serve with fragrant jasmine rice and pappadams.

3 Tbsp (45 mL) vegetable oil
2 cups (475 mL) paneer, cut into
 large cubes
2 Tbsp (30 mL) butter
2 tsp (10 mL) cumin seeds
1 tsp (5 mL) mustard seeds
½ tsp (2.5 mL) ground coriander
½ tsp (2.5 mL) ground cardamom

Half jalapeno pepper, diced
1 onion
3 cloves garlic, minced
2 Tbsp (30 mL) minced ginger
3 large tomatoes, roughly chopped
4 cups (1 L) shelled green peas
Juice of 1 lemon
Salt and pepper to taste

Heat oil in a large pan. Sear cubes of paneer in batches until golden. Drain on paper towel and set aside.

Melt butter in a skillet over medium heat. Add cumin and mustard seeds and cook until seeds begin to pop. Add coriander, cardamom and chili and cook until fragrant, about 1 minute. Add onion, garlic and ginger and cook until translucent and soft. Add tomatoes and reduce heat to low; simmer, stirring occasionally, for 10 minutes.

Add peas and cook just until vibrant green in colour, about 3 minutes (or 1 minute and 30 seconds if cooking from frozen). Add paneer, dress with lemon juice and season to taste with salt and pepper.

Yellow Split Pea Dahl

SERVES 4

Thick and satisfying, this mild curry is lovely served over rice or scooped up with naan and pappadams.

1 Tbsp (15 mL) olive oil

Half large onion, diced

2-inch (5-cm) piece ginger, minced

2 cloves garlic, minced

1 tsp (5 mL) turmeric

½ tsp (2.5 mL) cumin

½ tsp (2.5 mL) ground coriander

½ tsp (2.5 mL) red chili flakes

2½ cups (600 mL) Classic Garlic Broth, recipe on page 145 (or other vegetable stock)

1 tomato, diced

¼ cup (60 mL) finely chopped cilantro stems

1½ cups (350 mL) dry yellow split peas, rinsed and picked over

⅓ cup (80 mL) 3.5 percent milk

Salt and pepper

Steamed long-grain rice, naan or pappadams, for serving

¼ cup (60 mL) torn cilantro leaves, for garnish

Greek yogurt, for garnish

Heat olive oil in a large pot over medium heat. Add onion and cook until soft and translucent, about 5 minutes. Add ginger and garlic and cook 30 seconds. Add turmeric, cumin, coriander and red chili flakes. Stir constantly until spices become fragrant, about 1 minute. Add vegetable stock and tomato and lower heat to a simmer.

Add cilantro stems and split peas; bring to a boil, then cover and simmer until peas are soft, about 20 minutes. Remove from heat, add milk and season with salt and pepper.

Serve each portion atop steamed rice, or with naan and pappadams, and garnish with cilantro and a dollop of Greek yogurt.

Mac and Peas

SERVES 4

Mac and cheese devotees of all ages will never guess that their beloved cheese sauce has been replaced with this vegan version. In this recipe, puréed cashews and potatoes yield a creamy texture, while nutritional yeast provides a cheese-like flavour.

Vegan WITH EGG-FREE PASTA

SOURDOUGH CRUMB
1½ cups (350 mL) large cubes of stale sourdough bread
¼ cup (60 mL) olive oil
Salt and pepper

SAUCE
1 Tbsp (15 mL) olive oil
1 medium onion, cut into medium dice
2 garlic cloves, minced
½ tsp (2.5 mL) onion powder
½ tsp (2.5 mL) garlic powder
1 tsp (5 mL) mustard powder

¼ tsp (1 mL) crushed red pepper flakes
1 tsp (5 mL) paprika
⅓ cup (80 mL) nutritional yeast flakes
1 medium Yukon Gold potato, peeled and cut into small dice
¾ cup (180 mL) cooked navy beans
¾ cup (180 mL) raw cashews
1 cup (250 mL) water
1 Tbsp (15 mL) apple cider vinegar
Salt and pepper to taste
1 lb (455 g) dry pasta
1 cup (250 mL) shelled green peas

Preheat oven to 350F.

Pulse bread in the bowl of a food processor until fine crumbs have formed. Mix thoroughly with oil, season with salt and pepper, spread on a baking sheet and bake until golden brown. Wipe out bowl of food processor.

Bring a large pot of salted water to boil over high heat.

Continued on page 170

MAC AND PEAS CONTINUED

Heat olive oil in a medium pot. Add onion and cook until soft. Add garlic and cook until fragrant, about 30 seconds. Add spices, nutritional yeast, potato, beans and cashews to the pot. Add water, bring to a boil and cook, covered, until potatoes are tender and easily pierced with a knife, about 10 minutes.

Purée mixture in a high-powered blender or food processor with apple cider vinegar; season to taste with salt and pepper.

In the large pot of boiling water, cook pasta until al dente. Add peas for the last minute of cooking. Drain. Combine pasta, peas and sauce. Top with bread crumbs and serve.

Power Pulse Chili

SERVES 6

Whether you're preparing meals in advance or feeding a crowd, having a great chili recipe in your back pocket is a must. Serve with warm corn tortillas, queso fresco cheese and lime cheeks for spritzing.

3 Tbsp (45 mL) olive oil

1 onion, diced small

1 red pepper, diced small

5 cloves garlic, minced

1 jalapeno pepper, minced

1 tsp (5 mL) cumin

1 tsp (5 mL) Mexican oregano (or substitute regular oregano)

3 Tbsp (45 mL) ancho chili powder (or substitute regular chili powder)

1 tsp (5 mL) red chili pepper flakes

12-oz (341-mL) bottle light beer

3 Tbsp (45 mL) tomato paste

2 × 28-oz (796-mL) cans crushed tomatoes

1 Tbsp (15 mL) brown sugar

1 cup (250 mL) cooked pinto beans

2 cups (475 mL) cooked black beans

3 cups (710 mL) cooked kidney beans

2 Tbsp (30 mL) masa harina (corn flour)

2 tsp (10 mL) apple cider vinegar

Salt and pepper to taste

Heat oil in a large pot over medium heat. Sauté onion and red pepper until soft, about 6 minutes. Add garlic, jalapeno, cumin, oregano, chili powder and chili flakes. Cook until garlic is fragrant and spices are toasted. Deglaze pan with beer and stir in tomato paste, crushed tomatoes and brown sugar.

Pulse pinto beans in the bowl of a food processor until coarsely chopped.

Add all beans and masa harina to tomato base. Bring mixture to a boil and simmer until liquid is reduced and thickened, about 1 hour. Add vinegar and season to taste with salt and pepper.

Black Bean Empanadas

MAKES 8 TO 10

One cannot go wrong with bundles of flaky pastry wrapped around a warm, spicy filling. These empanadas can be made ahead of time and frozen before baking.

PASTRY

2¼ cups (530 mL) all-purpose flour

1½ tsp (7.5 mL) salt

½ cup (120 mL) cold unsalted butter, cubed

2 eggs, separated

⅓ cup (80 mL) ice water

1 Tbsp (15 mL) apple cider vinegar

1 Tbsp (15 mL) 35 percent cream

FILLING

2 cups (475 mL) dry black beans

1 onion, cut into medium dice

1 red bell pepper, cut into medium dice

2 cloves garlic, minced

1½ Tbsp (22.5 mL) tomato paste

1½ tsp (7.5 mL) cumin

1½ tsp (7.5 mL) hot smoked paprika

1 tsp (5 mL) dried oregano

2 cups (475 mL) grated Monterey jack cheese

¼ cup (60 mL) finely sliced scallions

In a food processor, combine flour and salt. Add butter and pulse until it is the consistency of small peas. In a separate bowl, whisk together 1 egg, water and vinegar. Slowly drizzle liquid through the feed tube until the mixture just comes together. Press dough into a disc, wrap in cling film and chill in the refrigerator for a minimum of 1 hour.

In a large pot, submerge beans under 3 inches (7.5 cm) of water. Add onion, red pepper, garlic, tomato paste, cumin, paprika and oregano. Cook

over high heat until the water comes to a boil. Reduce heat and allow to cook, uncovered, until beans are tender, about 1 hour and 30 minutes, adding water if beans become exposed. Drain and place in a medium bowl.

Add cheese and scallions to bean mixture and season to taste with salt and pepper.

Preheat oven to 400F (205C). Remove dough from fridge and roll out on a floured surface to ¼ inch (0.6 cm) in thickness. Cut dough into 6-inch (15-cm) circles and fill with 3 Tbsp (45 mL) of filling. Whisk remaining egg with cream. For each empanada, brush edges of dough with egg wash. Fold dough over into a crescent shape and pinch edges to seal. Brush empanadas with egg wash and bake until golden, about 25 minutes. Serve warm.

Spicy Black Beans with Broccoli and Cashews

SERVES 6

In this quick-to-prepare stir-fry, fermented black beans are used along with black turtle beans to add an extra depth of umami flavour.

¼ cup (60 mL) Classic Garlic Broth, recipe on page 145 (or other vegetable stock)

3 Tbsp (45 mL) Chinese rice wine (or substitute white wine or sherry)

1 Tbsp (15 mL) soy sauce

2 tsp (10 mL) cornstarch

1 tsp (5 mL) sugar

1 Tbsp (15 mL) canola oil

1-inch (2.5-cm) piece ginger, minced

1 cup (250 mL) cooked black beans

2 Tbsp (30 mL) fermented black beans (or substitute black bean sauce)

2 cloves garlic, minced

1½ lbs (680 g) rapini or broccoli rabe

½ cup (120 mL) whole cashews

2 tsp (10 mL) red chili oil

1 tsp (5 mL) sesame oil

Steamed rice, for serving

1 Tbsp (15 mL) black sesame seeds, for garnish

In a small bowl, stir stock, rice wine, soy sauce, cornstarch and sugar until cornstarch and sugar are dissolved.

In a wok or large sauté pan, heat oil over high heat. Add ginger and fry until fragrant, about 10 seconds. Add black beans, fermented beans and garlic. Add rapini and cashews and cook over high heat until rapini is al dente, about 3 to 4 minutes. Pour stock mixture over top and allow stock to reduce, about 1 minute. Toss in chili and sesame oils. Serve mixture atop rice and garnish with black sesame seeds.

Dan's Gluten-free Honey and Spice Bean Bread

MAKES 1 LOAF

Not only can pulses be ground into flour, they can be mashed and used to make a delicious loaf like this slightly sweet spice bread. See Grinding Gluten-free Flour from Pulses, page 24, for instructions on grinding your own flour from homegrown pulses.

½ cup (120 mL) butter or coconut oil
¼ cup (60 mL) honey
2 eggs
1½ cups (350 mL) cooked mild-flavoured beans, such as Ruckle, Swedish Brown or Nez Perce
1 ripe banana, mashed

¼ cup (60 mL) unsweetened applesauce
½ tsp (2.5 mL) salt
1¾ cups (415 mL) flour
2 tsp (10 mL) baking powder
1 tsp (5 mL) cinnamon
1 tsp (5 mL) nutmeg
½ tsp (2.5 mL) ground ginger

Preheat oven to 350F (180C). Butter and flour a standard loaf pan.

In a large bowl, cream butter or oil and honey. Beat in egg. In a separate bowl, mash beans with enough water or bean stock to make them moist but not soupy. Mix into egg mixture along with banana and applesauce.

Add dry ingredients to bean mixture and beat with hand mixer on high for about 4 minutes, or until mixture is well blended.

Pour batter into prepared loaf pan. Bake for 45 minutes or until a skewer inserted into the middle comes out clean. Turn out immediately onto a cooling rack.

Chickpea Peanut Butter Banana Cookies

MAKES ABOUT 2 DOZEN COOKIES

No one will guess that chickpeas are the secret ingredient in these kid-friendly (and wheat-free) treats.

⅓ cup (80 mL) rolled oats (not instant)

1 tsp (5 mL) baking powder

½ tsp (2.5 mL) baking soda

Pinch of salt

1½ cups (350 mL) cooked chickpeas, cooled

6 Tbsp (90 mL) unsalted butter, at room temperature

¾ cup (180 mL) granulated sugar

½ cup (120 mL) brown sugar

1 egg

¾ cup (180 mL) natural peanut butter

1 tsp (5 mL) vanilla extract

⅓ cup (80 mL) coarsely chopped peanuts

⅓ cup (80 mL) crushed banana chips

In the bowl of a food processor, pulse oats until a floury consistency is formed. Add baking powder, baking soda and salt, then pulse briefly to combine; transfer to a bowl and set aside.

Add chickpeas to food processor and process until a coarse meal is formed.

In the bowl of a stand mixer, cream butter with both sugars then whip until light in texture and pale in colour. Add chickpea meal, egg, peanut butter and vanilla extract, beating until combined.

Add dry ingredients to the peanut butter mixture and mix on low speed until combined. Fold in nuts and banana chips.

Chill dough in the fridge for at least 2 hours.

Preheat oven to 350F (180C). Scoop evenly sized balls onto parchment-lined baking sheet and bake until golden and set, about 12 minutes.

Black Bean Brownies with Espresso Ganache

MAKES 12 BROWNIES

Even the most dedicated brownie connoisseurs will be shocked to find out that this decadent dessert contains a hefty quantity of black beans, which are inherently mild in flavour. Lovely on their own, these brownies are taken to the next level with espresso ganache.

2 cups (475 mL) cooked black beans

6 oz (170 g) semi-sweet chocolate, melted

3 eggs

⅓ cup (80 mL) melted butter

¼ cup (60 mL) cocoa

1 Tbsp (15 mL) espresso powder (optional)

Pinch of salt

2 tsp (10 mL) vanilla

1 cup (250 mL) granulated sugar

ESPRESSO GANACHE

8 oz (225 g) semi-sweet chocolate

½ cup (120 mL) 35 percent cream

1 Tbsp (15 mL) maple syrup

1 tsp (5 mL) espresso powder (or instant coffee granules, dissolved in cream)

1 Tbsp (15 mL) unsalted butter

Preheat oven to 350F (180C).

Pulse beans in a food processor to form a paste. In a large bowl, combine beans and melted chocolate. Add remaining brownie ingredients and stir until combined. Pour batter into a greased 9-inch (22.5-cm) square pan and bake for about 25 minutes, or until a toothpick inserted into the centre comes out clean. Place pan on a rack and allow to cool completely before cutting.

For the ganache, melt chocolate over a double boiler. Add remaining ingredients and remove from heat. Allow mixture to cool before spreading over brownies.

Spiced Navy Bean Pumpkin Pie with Pecan Streusel

SERVES 8

Neutral in flavour and creamy in texture, navy beans are the secret ingredient in this version of traditional pumpkin pie. The beans combine with the pumpkin to give the filling a creamy texture. Pecan streusel topping provides a nice texture contrast to the smooth base.

PASTRY

1½ cups (350 mL) flour, plus more for dusting

½ cup (120 mL) unsalted butter, cubed and chilled

2 Tbsp (30 mL) granulated sugar

1 tsp (5 mL) salt

¼ cup (60 mL) ice-cold water

STREUSEL TOPPING

¾ cup (180 mL) coarsely chopped toasted pecans

¼ cup (60 mL) packed dark brown sugar

2 Tbsp (30 mL) all-purpose flour

½ tsp (2.5 mL) cinnamon

2 Tbsp (30 mL) unsalted butter

PIE FILLING

1 cup (250 mL) cooked navy beans

½ cup (120 mL) pumpkin purée

1 cup (250 mL) evaporated milk

1 cup (250 mL) granulated sugar

¼ cup (60 mL) unsalted butter, melted

1½ Tbsp (22.5 mL) flour

1 Tbsp (15 mL) vanilla extract

1 tsp (5 mL) ground cinnamon

½ tsp (2.5 mL) freshly grated nutmeg

3 eggs

In the bowl of a food processor, pulse flour, butter, sugar and salt into pea-sized crumbs. Add water and pulse until dough forms. Flatten dough into a disc and wrap in cling film. Chill dough for 1 hour.

Combine pecans, sugar, flour and cinnamon in a bowl. Using your fingertips, add the butter until coarse crumbs are formed. Set aside.

Preheat oven to 350F (180C).

Continued on page 182

SPICED NAVY BEAN PUMPKIN PIE WITH PECAN STREUSEL CONTINUED

In food processor, purée beans until smooth. In a large bowl, mix beans with remaining filling ingredients, stirring until combined.

On a lightly floured surface, roll dough into a 12-inch (30-cm) round. Fit dough into a 9-inch (22.5-cm) pie plate; trim edges and crimp. Pour filling into dough and top with streusel. Bake until golden brown on top and filling is set, about 1 hour. To test, wiggle the pie plate; if the centre of the filling only wiggles slightly, the filling is set. Let pie cool completely before serving.

ENDNOTES

1   Agri Exchange (http://agriexchange.apeda.gov.in/product_profile/Major_Exporing_Countries.aspx?categorycode=0305)

2   Watch the short online video *Pulses: The Food of the Future* to hear more about how pulses are integral to the future of growing food on this planet: http://www.pulsecanada.com/environment/videos

3   *Toronto Star* online (http://www.thestar.com/business/2012/02/08/this_food_of_the_future_could_be_next_big_thing_for_canada.html)

4   In 2013, the United Nations declared that 2016 will be the International Year of Pulses. (http://iyp2016.org/)

5   "Engineered Food and Your Health: The Nutritional Status of GMOs," a public lecture by Dr. Thierry Vrain at Trent University in Peterborough, ON, November 16, 2014.

6   *Wake Up Before It Is Too Late: Make Agriculture Truly Sustainable Now for Food Security in a Changing Climate*, the 2013 report by the United Nations Conference on Trade and Development, UNCTAD (http://unctad.org/en/PublicationsLibrary/ditcted2012d3_en.pdf)

7   "New UN Report Calls for Transformation in Agriculture," Institute for Agriculture and Trade Policy (http://www.iatp.org/blog/201309/new-un-report-calls-for-transformation-in-agriculture#sthash.gJbffl6z.dpuf)

8   The 68th UN General Assembly declared 2015 the International Year of Soils. (http://www.fao.org/soils-2015/about/)

9   Brenda Frick, "The Pulse of the Prairie," *The Canadian Organic Grower*, Spring 2006 (https://www.cog.ca/documents/PulsePrairieSP06.pdf)

10 Pulse Canada (http://www.pulsecanada.com/pulse-industry)

11 "Canadian Farms Getting Bigger, but Rarer," *CBC News* online (http://www.cbc.ca/news/business/canadian-farms-getting-bigger-but-rarer-1.1244248)

12 "In 1930, 1 out of every 3 Canadians lived on a farm. Today, only about 2 percent of the population live on farms." Career Bear (http://careerbear.com/farmer/article/farming-in-canada)

"There are over 313,000,000 people living in the United States. Of that population, less than 1 percent claim farming as an occupation (and about 2 percent actually live on farms)." United States Environmental Protection Agency (http://www.epa.gov/agriculture/ag101/demographics.html)

13 "World Food Day by the Numbers," USC CANADA (http://www.usc-canada.org/resources/news/item/171-world-food-day-by-the-numbers)

14 "Russian Family Gardens Produce 40% of Russian Food," *Health Impact News* (http://healthimpactnews.com/2014/russian-family-gardens-produce-40-of-russian-food/)

15 "Global Forum on Food Security and Nutrition," Food and Agriculture Organization of the United Nations (http://www.fao.org/fsnforum/)

16 In the US, for example, "GMOs are in as much as 80 percent of conventional processed food." Non GMO Project (http://www.nongmoproject.org/learn-more/)

17 Statistics Canada, "Canadian Agriculture at a Glance," 2014 (http://www.statcan.gc.ca/pub/96-325-x/2014001/article/11913-eng.htm)

"By 2012, 88% of corn and 94% of soy grown in the United States were genetically modified, according to the U.S. Department of Agriculture," "GMO Corn, Soybeans Dominate US Market," *IndustryWeek* (http://www.industryweek.com/supply-chain /gmo-corn-soybeans-dominate-us-market)

18 Dr. Mae-Wan Ho, "'Stunning' Difference of GM from Non-GM Corn," Permaculture Research Institute (http://permaculturenews .org/2013/04/22/stunning-difference-of-gm-from-non-gm-corn/)

19 David King et al., "Climate Change: A Risk Assessment," Centre for Science and Policy (http://www.csap.cam.ac.uk/projects /climate-change-risk-assessment/)

20 Lloyd's, *Food System Shock: The insurance impacts of acute disruption to global food supply*, Emerging Risk Report—2015 (http://www.lloyds .com/~/media/files/news%20and%20insight/risk%20insight/2015/food%20 system%20shock/food%20system%20shock_june%202015.pdf)

21 *Climate Change 2014: Impacts, Adaptation, and Vulnerability*, Intergovernmental Panel on Climate Change (http://www.ipcc.ch /report/ar5/wg2/)

22 "Pulses Are a 'Superfood'," Agriculture and Agri-Food Canada (http://www.pulsecanada.com/uploads/dI/y5/dIy5UDO9BpWjEAJb3YkQiA /Pulses-are-a-Superfood.pdf)

23 Mindy Hermann and Susan C. Male, "Bean Briefs," US Dry Bean Council, Spring 2014 (http://www.usdrybeans.com/wp-content/files/2014/04 /BeanBriefsSpring14web.pdf)

24 "Peas, Beans, Lentils and Cardiovascular Disease," Saskatchewan Pulse Growers (http://www.saskpulse.com/uploads/content/Pulses_and _Cardiovascular_Disease.pdf)

25 Megan A. McCrory et al., "Pulse Consumption, Satiety, and Weight Management." *Advances in Nutrition* 1(1), Nov 2010 (http://www.ncbi.nlm .nih.gov/pmc/articles/PMC3042778/)

26 "Pulses and the Gluten-Free Diet," Pulse Canada
(http://www.pulsecanada.com/pulses-and-the-gluten-free-diet)

27 Ibid.

28 Megan A. McCrory et al., "Pulse Consumption, Satiety, and Weight
Management," *Advances in Nutrition* 1(1), Nov 2010
(http://www.ncbi.nlm.nih.gov/pmc/articles/PMC3042778/)

29 "Food Security, Nutrition & Innovation," Global Pulse Confederation
(http://iyp2016.org/themes/food-security-nutrition-innovation)

30 "Protein Quality of Cooked Pulses," Pulse Canada (http://www
.pulsecanada.com/uploads/ff/28/ff28of2f10206d5a53a241ef6e2e2d25
/USA_PC_protein_fact_sheet_p6.pdf)

31 "Food Security, Nutrition & Innovation," Global Pulse Confederation
(http://iyp2016.org/themes/food-security-nutrition-innovation)

32 "Pulses and the Gluten-Free Diet," Pulse Canada
(http://www.pulsecanada.com/pulses-and-the-gluten-free-diet)

33 "Food Security, Nutrition & Innovation," Global Pulse Confederation
(http://iyp2016.org/themes/food-security-nutrition-innovation)

34 Irene Darmadi-Blackberry et al., "Legumes: The Most Important Dietary
Predictor of Survival in Older People of Different Ethnicities," *Asia Pacific
Journal of Clinical Nutrition,* 13 (2): 217–220 (http://apjcn.nhri.org.tw/server
/info/articles/diets-foods/Darmadi.pdf)

35 "Growing Field Peas in Alberta," Alberta Pulse Growers (http://pulse
.ab.ca/producers/varieties-management/peas/peas-overview)

36 Saskatchewan Pulse Growers (http://www.saskpulse.com/grow-buy-sell
/pulse-industry/)

INDEX

GARDENING INDEX
Page numbers in **bold** refer to photos

RECICE INDEX
Page numbers in **bold** refer to photos

ABOUT THE AUTHORS

Dan Jason lives on Salt Spring Island, BC, where he founded the mail-order seed company Salt Spring Seeds. He has written many bestselling books about growing and preparing food sustainably, including *The Whole Organic Food Book* and *Saving Seeds as if Our Lives Depended on It* (2006).

Hilary Malone holds a Diploma in Culinary Arts from Vancouver Island University and is co-owner (with Alison) of Sea Salt Food Company, a boutique catering and recipe development business.

Alison Malone Eathorne is a freelance travel and food writer and has contributed to various publications including *Pacific Yachting*, *Western Living* and *BC Home*.

Hilary and Alison are co-authors of the award-winning *Sea Salt: Recipes from the West Coast Galley* (Harbour, 2013). They live in Nanaimo, BC.